I0446243

Ocean Treasures Dropshipping: Your Ultimate Guide to Expanding Your Online Jewelry Business

Simplify Inventory Challenges, Overcome Cash Flow Obstacles
and Increase Sales with Powerful Dropship Leveraging!

but not limited to special, incidental, consequential, or other damages. As always, the advice of a competent legal, tax, accounting or other professional should be sought. The authors and publisher do not warrant the performance, effectiveness or applicability of any sites listed in this book. All links are for information purposes only and are not warranted for content, accuracy or any other implied or explicit purpose.

BOOK DESCRIPTION

Transform Your Struggling Watersports, Sea Life and Nautical Retail Jewelry Business! Take Your Online Store to the Next Level! With Peter Stone's "A High-Value Unique, Yet Simple and Profitable, Worldwide Delivery, Dropship Jewelry Program".

Get noticed while you expand your online store presence in a big way. This revolutionary approach to niche market jewelry sales will add massive value with many different jewelry collections that will skyrocket your online sales and dominate the market.

Imagine this: you no longer need to worry about inventory control, no more headaches, and no more excess inventory. Peter Stone's program will show you exactly how to grow your jewelry business with a niche line of finely detailed jewelry and over 6500 unique designs to choose from in 43+ niche market collections. You will make excellent sales and outstanding profits by selling and marketing your unique DiveSilver jewelry designs in sterling silver and high-value, high-profit 14, 18, or 22Kt gold jewelry.

With this program, you can make the move from a fixed store to an online cyber inventory store with little to no stocking costs, saving you time and money. You can succeed without all the hassle of managing inventory and dealing with tight cash flow. Here's what you can gain from the program:

• Zero Inventory – easy to add and take away images in your store

• No Inventory Headaches – simple to measure and manage data

• Free up your time and your cash – make more money

Don't wait any longer to take your nautical, sea life and watersports retail jewelry business and online store to the next level. With Peter Stone's "A High-Value Unique, Yet Simple and Profitable, Deliver Anywhere, Drop Shipping Jewelry Program," you can save time managing inventory and make more money with increased marketing efforts by spending more time at the marketing and sales desks. Get this book now and start boosting your sales with mid-level and high-end ocean sports, sea life and nautical retail fun and feel-good jewelry!

TABLE OF CONTENTS:

Chapter 7
Flow with the Dropshipping Tides: Staying Ahead with Trends in Sea Life and Ocean Sports Retail Jewelry Sales

Chapter 8
From Ocean to E-commerce: Conquer the Market with the Addition of Expanded Dropship Online

Chapter 9
Mastering Success: Essential Steps for Implementing Effective Dropshipping Strategies

CHAPTER 1
Maximizing Choices: Unleash the Power of Inventory Management Strategies

CHAPTER 2
Unveiling the Jewelry Revolution: Businesses Thriving with Dropshipping Services

CHAPTER 3
Bring the Brilliance: Unlocking Success with Precious Metals in Sea Life and Ocean Sports Retail

CHAPTER 4
Dive into Success: Unveiling Targeted Collections in Ocean Sports Jewelry Retail

CHAPTER 5

Anchoring Quality: Ensuring Reliability and Excellence in Dropshipping Jewelry

CHAPTER 6
Tracking Dropshipping Triumph: Essential Metrics for Dropship Virtual Inventory Management Success

CHAPTER 7
Flow with the Dropshipping Tides: Staying Ahead with Trends in Sea Life and Ocean Sports Retail Jewelry Sales

CHAPTER 8

From Ocean to E-commerce: Conquer the Market with the Addition of Expanded Dropship Online

CHAPTER 9
Mastering Success: Essential Steps for Implementing Effective Dropshipping Strategies

INTRODUCTION:

Hey there, struggling dive, ocean sports, sea life jewelry store owners, operators and managers! Congratulations on purchasing my latest book, "Ocean Treasures Dropshipping: The Ultimate Guide to Making Money with Luxurious Nautical, Sea Life, and Water-sports Jewelry." You've taken a big step towards unlocking the secrets of boosting your online sales and dominating the market in the world of ocean sports, sea life, and nautical retail jewelry.

Running a business in this industry can be overwhelming. Inventory control, cash flow management, and constantly staying on top of the latest trends can consume much of your time and energy. But fear not! With the knowledge and strategies shared in this book, you'll be able to significantly reduce your workload, stress, and overwhelm, giving you more time for what truly matters – focused jewelry design, sales, and proper marketing.

As someone with deep expertise in ocean sports and the jewelry industry, including being an Ocean Sports and world Adventurer, Captain 100 Ton, Chief Engineer Merchant Ships, C.E.O. of Int'l Jewelry Manufacturing Est. 1987, Author, Speaker, Master Coach and Consultant, and Gemologist; G.G., A.G., F.G.A., I am uniquely positioned to guide you through this journey.

Inside this book, you'll find practical advice, tips, tricks, and real-life examples that will help you master the art of dropshipping luxurious nautical, sea life, and water sports jewelry. I'll provide you with the knowledge and tools to expand your business in a big way by offering a wide selection of products that will blow your customers away.

One of the biggest advantages of dropshipping is avoiding the hassle of managing inventory control and dealing with tight cash flow. With dropshipping, you don't need to worry about stocking up on inventory or packaging and shipping products. You can focus on what you do best – providing exceptional customer service, designing beautiful jewelry, and growing your business.

But dropshipping is more than just setting up an online store and listing products. In this book, I'll walk you through the entire process, from finding reliable suppliers to marketing and driving traffic to your online store. You'll learn how to curate a selection of high-quality, mid-level to high-end ocean sports, sea life, and nautical retail jewelry that will captivate your target audience.

Imagine standing out in the market with a wide variety of luxurious nautical, sea life, and water sports jewelry that your competitors cannot match. With the insights provided in this book, you'll be able to offer your customers a unique and unforgettable shopping experience, ensuring their loyalty and driving repeat sales.

So, what are you waiting for? Dive into the pages of "Ocean Treasures Dropshipping" and start implementing the strategies and techniques shared within. You already have the book in your hands, so let's make the most of it! By the end, you'll be equipped with the knowledge and confidence to reduce your workload, stress, and overwhelm, allowing you to focus on what truly matters – creating beautiful jewelry, increasing sales, and dominating the market.

Get ready to transform your business and make waves in the world of ocean sports, sea life, and nautical retail jewelry. The journey starts now!

BIOGRAPHY

Unlock Your Maximum Potential: Peter Stone - Ocean Sports Enthusiast & World Adventurer, Captain 100 Ton, Chief Engineer Merchant Ships, CEO Int'l Jewelry Manufacturing Est. 1987, Author, Speaker, Master Coach and Consultant, Gemologist; G.G, A.G., F.G.A. - Is Here to Help Struggling Dive, Ocean Sports, Sea Life Gift and Resort Online Store Owners Reach Their Goals!

Are you an ocean/beach/dive resort online store owner struggling to get noticed while working to expand in a big way? By adding unparalleled value through an extensive range of jewelry collections in both fine sterling silver and gold jewelry that will skyrocket your online sales and dominate the market Is the Solution! You need to Look no further because the solution is the book you hold in your hands.

Peter Stone has the experience and knowledge to help you reach your goals. As a Graduate A.G. of the Asian Gemological Institute of Sciences, Graduate Gemologist G.G. – High Honors, GIA, F.G.A. of the Gemological Association of Great Britain, and having an extensive diamond study at I.G.I. - Antwerp, Belgium, Peter has been working in the world's gemstone cutting and jewelry manufacturing center of Bangkok, Thailand, since 1987. For over 30 years, Peter has been designing, manufacturing, and selling jewelry, and traveling to, studying, observing and selling at jewelry shows and trade fairs worldwide since 1985. He has also managed, designed, and overseen Jewelry manufacturing, marketing, copywriting, and sales since 1992 and trained a staff of over 100 individuals to produce detailed, fine-quality jewelry.

With thousands of exclusive designs, collections, and one-of-a-kind creations for customers and high-level clients worldwide in over 43+ niche markets, including Fine Nautical, Sea Life and Ocean Collections, Peter has the knowledge and skills to help you skyrocket your online sales. He is also experienced in jewelry export, wholesale, retail, and dropship business models.

He has owned and operated over 18 retail gift and jewelry stores worldwide and implemented and operated over 33 online wholesale and retail businesses under a number of brands. As a coffee roaster and restauranteur, Key West shrimper, whale watch and tour boat captain, scuba diver, swimmer, open ocean wave runner enthusiast, rower, and bicyclist, Peter has a wealth of knowledge, energy, and experience to help you reach your goals.

That's why Peter wrote the book "Ocean Treasures Dropshipping: The Ultimate Guide to Making Money with Luxurious Nautical, Sea Life, and Water-sports Jewelry." This book is the perfect tool to help you unlock your maximum potential and get noticed. At the same time, you expand big by adding massive value through extensive selections that will skyrocket your online sales and dominate the market.

So what are you waiting for? Start reading "Ocean Treasures Dropshipping: The Ultimate Guide to Making Money with Luxurious Nautical, Sea Life, and Water-sports Jewelry" right now and join Peter Stone on social media to get even more tips and advice on how to reach your goals.

CHAPTER 1. MAXIMIZING CHOICES: UNLEASH THE POWER OF INVENTORY MANAGEMENT STRATEGIES

"The dropshipping revolution allows businesses to expand their horizons without expanding their warehouses."

- "Discover the secrets to reducing inventory levels while providing customers with an expanded range of choices."
- "Unlock the power of data analytics to accurately forecast demand and make informed inventory decisions, cutting your buying errors and selling more."
- "Revolutionize your business model with dropshipping - expand your offerings without the need for physical inventory management or storage."
- "Harness the power of technology to improve inventory tracking and eliminate stockouts and overstock situations."
- "Transform your business with suppliers through vendor-managed inventory reporting - always have the right jewelry in stock without excessive inventory."

In order to successfully reduce inventory levels while maintaining a wide range of choices for customers, several strategies can be implemented. These strategies are aimed at improving inventory management efficiency, enhancing forecasting accuracy, and optimizing jewelry collection selections and procurement processes. Below are some of the most effective methods that have yielded positive results:

1. Implementing Just-in-Time (JIT) inventory management: JIT

is a concept that aims to minimize inventory levels by receiving goods and materials just in time for production or sale. By closely monitoring customer demand patterns and collaborating with suppliers for timely deliveries, excessive inventory can be eliminated, reducing holding costs and the risk of obsolescence.

2. Utilizing data-driven demand forecasting: Implementing advanced inventory management systems that leverage Dropshipping analytics can significantly improve forecasting accuracy. Businesses can make more informed decisions regarding jewelry assortment and quantities by analyzing historical sales data, trending patterns, and market trends. Accurate demand forecasting ensures that the right Jewelry designs are available in the right quantities, in both Fine Sterling Silver and 14 and 18 Kt gold options, minimizing excess inventory.

3. Adopting dropshipping as a fulfillment model: Dropshipping allows businesses to expand their product offerings without the need for physical inventory storage. By partnering with reliable suppliers and manufacturers, items can be shipped directly to customers, reducing the need for warehousing and associated costs. This approach enables businesses to offer a wider range of choices while maintaining lean inventory levels.

4. Leveraging technology for better inventory tracking: Implementing inventory management software can provide real-time visibility into stock levels, enabling businesses to track inventory movement and plan reordering more efficiently. You will minimize stockouts and overstock situations by utilizing automated systems like dropship sales data reports that allow for vastly improved wholesale inventory purchase accuracy.

5. Collaborating with suppliers and adopting vendor-managed inventory (VMI): VMI allows suppliers to have increased visibility into customer demand, taking responsibility for inventory replenishment decisions. By establishing solid partnerships with

suppliers and sharing sales data, businesses can ensure that they always have the right products in stock, reducing the need for excessive inventory.

In conclusion, reducing inventory levels while maintaining a wide range of choices for customers requires a comprehensive approach that combines effective inventory management techniques, accurate dropshipping demand forecasting, strategic use of technology, and collaboration with suppliers. By implementing these strategies, businesses can achieve optimal inventory levels, vastly improve cash flow, and enhance customer satisfaction.

Now that we have discussed the most effective strategies for reducing inventory levels while maintaining a wide range of choices for customers, it's time to take a closer look at how these strategies can be implemented. I have created a checklist that will help you ensure you are following these strategies and maximizing their benefits.

Checklist

Problem-Solving Checklist for Inventory Management and Customer Choice:

1. Evaluate current inventory management system: Assess the efficiency and effectiveness of the current inventory management system in place. Identify any bottlenecks, inefficiencies, or areas for improvement.

2. Identify customer demand patterns: Analyze historical sales data to identify customer demand patterns. Determine which products are high-demand and which are low-demand.

3. Implement Just-in-Time (JIT) inventory management: Explore the feasibility of implementing JIT practices to reduce inventory levels with your jewelry supplier. Monitor customer demand patterns closely and collaborate with suppliers for timely

deliveries.

4. Utilize data-driven demand forecasting: Implement advanced inventory management systems leveraging data-automated analytics to improve accuracy. Analyze historical sales data, trending patterns, and market trends to make informed decisions regarding product assortment and quantities.

5. Consider dropshipping as a fulfillment model: Explore the possibility of adopting dropshipping as a fulfillment model to expand jewelry offerings without the need for physical inventory storage. Partner with reliable suppliers and manufacturers for direct shipment to customers.

6. Leverage technology for better inventory tracking: Implement inventory, easy-to-use management software that provides real-time visibility into stock levels. Utilize automated systems like barcode scanning and RFID tagging to improve inventory accuracy, minimizing stockouts and overstock situations.

7. Continuously monitor and adjust strategies: Regularly assess the effectiveness of implemented strategies and make necessary adjustments. Monitor customer demand, sales data, and inventory levels to ensure optimal inventory management and customer satisfaction.

8. Offer customized design services to your customers in-store and online. It's a great way to build sales and get free word-of-mouth advertising. It is perfect for gift-giving holidays and special occasions.

By following this problem-solving checklist, businesses can effectively reduce inventory levels while maintaining a wide range of selections for customers. They can enhance inventory management efficiency, improve forecasting accuracy, optimize product selection and procurement processes, and ultimately improve customer satisfaction and cash flow while they build more sales.

Now that we have reviewed this problem-solving checklist for inventory management and customer choice, let's take a look at some examples that demonstrate how these strategies can be implemented in a real-life scenario.

Examples

Here are several examples to illustrate the points made:

1. Example for JIT inventory management:
A clothing manufacturer closely monitors customer demand patterns and collaborates with fabric suppliers for timely deliveries. They receive fabric just in time for production, minimizing the need for excessive inventory. This strategy helps reduce holding costs and the risk of outdated styles.

2. Example for data-driven demand forecasting:
An online retailer uses an advanced inventory management system to analyze historical sales data, trending patterns, and market trends. Based on this analysis, they make informed decisions about which products to stock and in what quantities. This ensures that they meet customer demand without carrying unnecessary inventory.

3. Example for dropshipping as a fulfillment model:
A home goods store partners with various suppliers and manufacturers who handle fulfillment. When a customer places an order, the supplier ships the item directly to the customer. This eliminates the need for the store to hold inventory, allowing them to offer a broader range of products without the associated costs.

4. Example for better inventory tracking:
A specialty gift and jewelry store implements a cost-effective inventory management software that provides real-time visibility into stock levels. Using barcode scanning combined with online sales, they accurately track inventory movement, automatically triggering reordering when stock levels are low. This helps

prevent out-of-stock situations and minimizes excess inventory.

5. Example for collaborating with suppliers and VMI:
An electronics retailer establishes a strong supplier partnership and shares sales data with them. Based on this information, the suppliers take responsibility for replenishing inventory, ensuring that the retailer always has the right products in stock. This reduces the need for excessive inventory and improves supply chain efficiency.

These examples demonstrate how different strategies can be implemented to reduce inventory levels while offering customers a wide range of choices.

Now that we have examined several examples of inventory management strategies, let's dive into a case study that showcases how a company successfully implemented these strategies to optimize their inventory levels and improve their overall supply chain efficiency.

Case Study

Case Study: Ocean Jewelry Co. - Implementing a Unique Dropshipping Service

Background:
Ocean Jewelry Co. is a retail jewelry company specializing in mid-level and high-end ocean sports, sea life, and nautical jewelry gifts. The company faced the challenge of maintaining a wide range of choices for customers while reducing inventory levels to improve efficiency and reduce holding costs. To address this challenge, Ocean Jewelry Co. implemented various strategies based on the key points discussed in the article.

Key Strategies Implemented:

1. Just-in-Time (JIT) Inventory Management: Ocean Jewelry Co. closely monitored customer demand patterns and collaborated with suppliers to ensure timely deliveries. They adopted a JIT

approach to minimize inventory levels and reduce the risk of obsolescence. This strategy helped eliminate excessive inventory and holding costs.

2. Data-Driven Demand Forecasting: The company implemented advanced inventory management systems that leveraged data analytics. Ocean Jewelry Co. improved forecasting accuracy by analyzing historical dropship and in-store sales data, trending patterns, and market trends. This forecasting enabled them to make informed decisions regarding product assortment and quantities, minimizing excess inventory.

3. Dropshipping Fulfillment Model: Ocean Jewelry Co. adopted dropshipping as a fulfillment model. They partnered with a reliable supplier and manufacturer, allowing items to be shipped directly to customers. This partnership eliminated the need for physical inventory storage, reducing warehousing costs. The dropshipping model enabled the company to offer a broader range of choices while maintaining lean inventory levels.

4. Technology-Enabled Inventory Tracking: Ocean Jewelry Co. implemented inventory management software with real-time visibility into stock levels. They utilized barcode scanning and RFID tagging combined with online sales data for improved inventory accuracy. This technology allowed them to track inventory movement and plan reordering more efficiently, minimizing stockouts and overstock situations.

5. Supplier Collaboration & Vendor-Managed Inventory (VMI): The company established strong partnerships with suppliers and implemented a vendor-managed inventory system. Through VMI, suppliers had increased visibility into customer demand and took responsibility for inventory replenishment decisions. By sharing sales data with suppliers, Ocean Jewelry Co. ensured that they always had the right products in stock, reducing the need for excessive inventory.

Measurable Outcomes:

1. Reduced Inventory Levels: Ocean Jewelry Co. successfully reduced inventory levels by effectively implementing JIT inventory management and dropshipping. This process led to significant cost savings on holding inventory.

2. Increased Jewelry Selection: By adopting dropshipping, the company was able to expand its product offerings without the need for physical inventory storage. This Dropshipping strategy resulted in a wider range of choices for customers, leading to increased sales and customer satisfaction.

3. Improved Forecasting Accuracy: The implementation of data-driven demand forecasting systems improved forecasting accuracy, ensuring the availability of the right products in the right quantities. This minimized excess inventory and reduced the risk of stockouts.

Challenges Faced:

1. Supplier Collaboration: Establishing strong partnerships and implementing VMI required effective communication and supplier cooperation. Building trust and sharing data were challenges initially but were overcome through mutual benefits and long-term relationships.

2. Technology Implementation: Implementing inventory management software and barcode scanning systems required training and initial investment in technology. Overcoming technological challenges and ensuring system integration were crucial for successful implementation. Their vendor was knowledgeable in this area and provided simple, cost-effective solutions.

Lessons Learned:

1. Collaboration is Key: Building strong partnerships and collaborating with suppliers is essential for successful inventory management. Sharing data and aligning goals can lead to efficient

inventory replenishment and improved customer satisfaction.

2. Technology Enhancements: Investing in inventory management software and technology-enabled tracking systems can significantly improve efficiency and accuracy. Continuous improvement and adaptation of technology are essential for long-term success.

3. Embracing Dropshipping: Adopting the dropshipping model allowed Ocean Jewelry Co. to expand its product range, reduce inventory levels, and increase customer satisfaction. Embracing innovative fulfillment models can lead to sustainable growth and cost savings.

Overall Impact and Assessment:

Ocean Jewelry Co. successfully reduced inventory levels while expanding their business by implementing a comprehensive approach combining effective inventory management techniques, data-driven forecasting, technology-enabled tracking systems, and collaboration with suppliers. The dropshipping model played a significant role in achieving this outcome, allowing them to deliver worldwide and offer a wide range of choices. The company experienced cost savings, improved cash flow, and enhanced customer satisfaction. The strategies implemented have proven to be effective and sustainable, positioning Ocean Jewelry Co. for future growth and success.

Now that we have examined the case study of Ocean Jewelry Co.'s successful implementation of various strategies to improve efficiency and reduce holding costs, let's take a look at some of the mistakes to avoid when implementing similar initiatives.

Typical Mistakes And How To Avoid Them

Based on the material covered, here are some common mistakes people make in inventory management and how they can be avoided:

1. Keeping excessive inventory: Many businesses make the mistake of holding excessive stock, which ties up capital and increases holding costs. This can be avoided by implementing just-in-time (JIT) inventory management, closely monitoring customer demand patterns, and collaborating with suppliers for timely deliveries.

2. Poor demand forecasting: Inaccurate demand forecasting can lead to overstocking or stockouts. To avoid this, businesses should utilize data-driven demand forecasting by leveraging advanced inventory management systems that analyze historical sales data, trending patterns, and market trends.

3. Mismanaging inventory tracking: Without proper inventory tracking, it becomes challenging to make informed decisions and plan reordering efficiently. Businesses can improve inventory accuracy and minimize stockouts and overstock situations by leveraging technology, such as inventory management software with real-time visibility and automated systems like barcode scanning and RFID tagging.

4. Neglecting the advantages of dropshipping: Many businesses overlook the benefits of dropshipping as a fulfillment model. By partnering with reliable suppliers and manufacturers, companies can ship items directly to customers, eliminating the need for physical inventory storage and associated costs.

5. Lack of collaboration with suppliers: Failing to collaborate with suppliers and share sales data can result in a mismatch between inventory levels and customer demand. Adopting vendor-managed inventory (VMI) can help businesses establish strong partnerships with suppliers, allowing them to have increased visibility into customer demand and ensuring the availability of the right products in stock.

By avoiding these common mistakes and implementing the strategies mentioned, businesses can achieve optimal inventory levels, improve cash flow, and enhance customer satisfaction.

After learning about these common mistakes to avoid in inventory management, it is essential to focus on the #1 piece of advice to mitigate these risks and improve overall inventory management effectively.

My #1 Piece Of Advice

My top advice for struggling dive, sea life, ocean sports, and beach resort shops with online stores is to consider reducing inventory levels and implementing a unique dropshipping service for sterling silver, 14K, 18K, and 22K gold jewelry. This service will allow you to expand your business while offering customers a wide range of nautical retail jewelry gifts worldwide. By leveraging a reliable dropshipping model, you can reduce the risk of excess inventory and focus on providing exceptional products and services with exponentially increased sales.

Summary:

- Implement Just-in-Time (JIT) inventory management to minimize excess inventory, reduce holding costs, and eliminate the risk of obsolescence.
- Improve forecasting accuracy by implementing data-driven demand forecasting systems that analyze historical sales data and market trends.
- Expand product offerings without physical inventory storage through dropshipping, partnering with reliable suppliers for direct shipments to customers.
- Utilize inventory management software and automated systems like barcode scanning and RFID tagging for real-time visibility and improved inventory accuracy.
- Enhance collaboration with suppliers and adopt vendor-managed inventory (VMI) to ensure optimal stock levels and reduce the need for excessive inventory.

Quiz

Questions:
1. What is Just-in-Time (JIT) inventory management?
2. What is the benefit of utilizing data-driven demand forecasting?
3. How does dropshipping enable businesses to maintain lean inventory levels?
4. What technology can be used to improve inventory tracking?
5. How does vendor-managed inventory (VMI) allow businesses to reduce the need for excessive inventory?
6. What is the purpose of implementing effective inventory management techniques?
7. How can businesses improve cash flow by reducing inventory levels?
8. How can businesses ensure they always have the right products in stock?
9. What is the main benefit of adopting dropshipping as a fulfillment model?
10. What is the overall goal of implementing strategies to reduce inventory levels?

Answer Key:
1. Just-in-Time (JIT) inventory management is a concept that aims to minimize inventory levels by receiving goods and materials just in time for production or sale.
2. Utilizing data-driven demand forecasting can significantly improve forecasting accuracy by analyzing historical sales data, trending patterns, and market trends.
3. Dropshipping allows businesses to expand their product offerings without the need for physical inventory storage by having items shipped directly to customers.
4. Technology such as inventory management software, barcode scanning, and RFID tagging can be used to improve inventory tracking.

5. Vendor-managed inventory (VMI) allows suppliers to have increased visibility into customer demand, taking responsibility for inventory replenishment decisions.

6. implementing effective inventory management techniques aims to improve inventory management efficiency, enhance forecasting accuracy, and optimize product selection and procurement processes.

7. Businesses can improve cash flow by reducing inventory levels eliminating holding costs and the risk of obsolescence.

8. Businesses can ensure they always have the right products in stock by collaborating with suppliers and adopting vendor-managed inventory (VMI).

9. The main benefit of adopting dropshipping as a fulfillment model is that it reduces the need for warehousing and associated costs.

10. The overall goal of implementing strategies to reduce inventory levels is to maintain a wide range of choices for customers while minimizing holding costs and the risk of obsolescence.

Now that we understand the key strategies for reducing inventory levels without compromising on product options, let's dive into some inspiring success stories of retail jewelry businesses that have successfully implemented a dropshipping service. This exciting approach allows for a wide range of choices while minimizing inventory risks. Keep reading to discover how these businesses thrived and find inspiration for your own journey!

CHAPTER 2. UNVEILING THE JEWELRY REVOLUTION: BUSINESSES THRIVING WITH DROPSHIPPING SERVICES

"Ocean Jewels went from a sinking ship to a thriving treasure chest with dropshipping!"

- "Discover how Ocean Jewels, a beach resort jewelry giftshop, skyrocketed their success by incorporating dropshipping into their business model."
- "From limited stock availability to high inventory costs, learn how dropshipping helped Ocean Jewels overcome numerous business obstacles."
- "Find out how dropshipping enabled Ocean Jewels to greatly expand their product range, offering a wide selection of jewelry gifts for diverse customer preferences."
- "Learn how dropshipping reduced overhead costs for Ocean Jewels, allowing them to allocate more funds towards marketing efforts and driving increased sales."
- "Explore how dropshipping improved order fulfillment for Ocean Jewels, leading to faster shipping and enhanced customer satisfaction."

Absolutely! There have been numerous businesses that have achieved great success by implementing a dropshipping service for their retail jewelry gifts. One notable success story is that of Ocean Jewels, a beach resort jewelry giftshop that experienced tremendous growth after incorporating dropshipping into their business model.

Before implementing dropshipping, Ocean Jewels faced several challenges, including limited stock availability, high inventory costs, and the inability to offer a wide selection of products to their customers. However, by leveraging the dropshipping model, they were able to overcome these obstacles and achieve significant results.

First and foremost, dropshipping allowed Ocean Jewels to greatly expand their product range. By partnering with multiple reputable suppliers, they gained access to a much wider selection of jewelry gifts, including mid-level to high-end options. This enabled them to cater to a broader range of customers with diverse tastes and preferences, making their store more attractive to potential buyers.

Moreover, by eliminating the need to hold inventory, Ocean Jewels significantly reduced their overhead costs. They no longer needed to invest in large quantities of stock upfront, which helped improve their cash flow and overall financial stability. This cost-saving benefit allowed them to allocate more funds towards marketing efforts, driving more traffic to their online store and increasing their sales.

Additionally, dropshipping provided Ocean Jewels with the ability to fulfill customer orders more efficiently and promptly. Instead of relying on their own storage and shipping infrastructure, they leveraged their suppliers' logistics capabilities. This allowed for faster order processing and shipping, leading to improved customer satisfaction and increased customer loyalty.

Furthermore, by implementing a dropshipping service, Ocean Jewels enhanced their online presence and visibility. They were able to collaborate with their suppliers to create high-quality product images and descriptions, ensuring that their online store showcased the beauty and uniqueness of each jewelry gift. Coupled with well-executed digital marketing strategies, this led to increased brand awareness, higher website traffic, and ultimately, more sales.

In conclusion, the success story of Ocean Jewels demonstrates the immense benefits that businesses can derive from implementing a dropshipping service for their retail jewelry gifts. By expanding their product range, reducing overhead costs, improving order fulfillment, and enhancing their online presence, they were able to attract more customers, increase sales, and establish themselves as a dominant player in the market. If other struggling dive, surf, ocean sports beach resort sea life jewelry giftshops want to achieve similar success, adopting dropshipping could be a game-changing strategy.

Now that we have explored the success story of Ocean Jewels and the benefits they obtained from implementing dropshipping, it's time to dive deeper into how other dive, surf, ocean sports beach resort sea life jewelry giftshops can achieve similar results. To help you get started, I have created a comprehensive checklist that outlines the key steps and considerations for incorporating dropshipping into your business model.

Checklist

Preparations Checklist for Implementing Dropshipping for Retail Jewelry Gifts:

1. Research and identify a proven, reputable supplier in the jewelry industry that offer eceptional dropshipping services. Look for suppliers that have a wide range of products and offer good quality jewelry gifts.

2. Analyze your current inventory and identify the products that are in high demand and those that are not selling well. Determine the gaps in your product range that can be filled through dropshipping.

3. Evaluate your current financial situation and calculate the potential cost savings from eliminating the need to hold inventory. Determine how these savings can be allocated towards marketing efforts to increase sales.

4. Develop a marketing strategy that focuses on driving more

traffic to your online store. Consider utilizing digital marketing techniques such as search engine optimization (SEO), social media marketing, and email marketing to enhance your online presence and increase brand awareness.

5. Collaborate with your chosen suppliers to create high-quality product images and descriptions that showcase the beauty and uniqueness of each jewelry gift. This will help attract customers and persuade them to make a purchase.

6. Ensure that your website is optimized for easy navigation and user-friendly experience. Make sure that it is mobile responsive and has a secure payment gateway to instill trust and confidence in customers.

7. Implement a reliable order fulfillment process by leveraging your suppliers' logistics capabilities. Establish clear agreements with your suppliers regarding order processing and shipping times to ensure prompt delivery and customer satisfaction.

8. Train your customer service team to handle customer inquiries and complaints efficiently. Provide them with the necessary information about your dropshipping suppliers and their products so that they can assist customers effectively.

9. Monitor and evaluate the performance of your dropshipping service regularly. Keep track of sales, customer feedback, and any issues that may arise. Make adjustments and improvements to your dropshipping strategy as needed.

10. Continuously update your jewelry collections by exploring new designs and special niche markets plus adding trending jewelry gifts in Gold. Stay updated with industry trends and customer preferences to ensure that your jewelry offerings remain relevant and appealing.

By following this checklist, businesses can properly prepare for implementing dropshipping for their retail jewelry gifts, similar to the success story of Ocean Jewels.

Now that we have gone through the checklist for implementing dropshipping for retail jewelry gifts, let's take a look at some examples that align with each of the checklist items.

Examples

Here are a few additional examples to help illustrate the benefits of dropshipping for retail jewelry giftshops:

1. Sparkling Seas Boutique:
Sparkling Seas Boutique is a small, local jewelry giftshop that struggled with limited resources and inventory. By implementing a dropshipping service, they were able to dramatically expand their collections and offer a wider selection of jewelry options, including customizable pieces. This attracted a larger customer base and increased their sales, ultimately allowing them to open a second location. When they added the gold jewelry to their store that's when their business really took off!

2. Elegant Treasures:
Elegant Treasures, an established jewelry giftshop, faced the challenge of managing inventory costs and management systems. By partnering with a proven, reputable dropshipping supplier, they were able to eliminate these issues and reduce their overhead costs significantly. This freed up resources that they could reinvest in marketing efforts, resulting in increased brand exposure and a big boost in their online sales.

3. Gemstone Gallery:
Gemstone Gallery, an online jewelry retailer, struggled with slow order processing and shipping times due to their lack of a dedicated logistics infrastructure. By integrating a dropshipping service into their business model, they were able to leverage their suppliers' efficient fulfillment processes, leading to faster delivery and improved customer satisfaction. This resulted in higher customer retention rates and positive reviews, further enhancing their reputation and driving more sales.

4. Nature's Charms:

Nature's Charms, a nature-themed jewelry giftshop, wanted to expand their product offerings to include eco-friendly and sustainable jewelry options. By partnering with eco-conscious dropshipping suppliers, they were able to source and offer a wide range of environmentally friendly jewelry pieces. This not only aligned with their brand values but also attracted a niche customer base that valued sustainability, resulting in increased sales and brand loyalty.

5. Jewel Fusions:

Jewel Fusions, a jewelry giftshop that specialized in unique, handcrafted pieces, struggled with marketing and reaching a wider audience beyond their local market. By collaborating with a solid dropshipping supplier who had established online platforms and a strong customer base, they were able to expand their reach and sell their products to customers worldwide. This global exposure led to a significant increase in sales and helped established Jewel Fusions as a reputable brand in the industry.

Now that we have explored several examples of how dropshipping has benefited retail jewelry giftshops, let's dive into a case study that further illustrates the advantages of implementing a dropshipping service.

Case Study

Case Study: Ocean Jewels - Transforming a Beach Resort Jewelry Giftshop through Dropshipping

Overview: Ocean Jewels is a beach resort jewelry giftshop that experienced exceptional growth by incorporating dropshipping into their business model. Prior to implementing dropshipping, the company faced challenges with limited stock availability, high inventory costs, and a restricted product range.

Challenges Faced:

1. Limited stock availability: Ocean Jewels struggled to maintain a diverse inventory due to upfront investment in stock.

2. High inventory costs: Holding a large quantity of stock required significant financial investment, impacting their cash flow.

3. Restricted jewelry collection: The limited product range made it challenging to cater to a diverse customer base and meet their preferences and tastes.

Actions Taken:

1. Partnered with a reputable supplier: By collaborating with an experienced reputable supplier, 20+ years dropshipping experience, Ocean Jewels gained access to a wider selection of jewelry gifts, including mid-level to high-end options including gold which they could have never afforded to stock.

2. Implemented dropshipping model: By leveraging the dropshipping model, Ocean Jewels eliminated the need for inventory and time to manage stock, reducing overhead costs and improving cash flow.

3. Enhanced online presence: Collaborating with their supplier, Ocean Jewels created high-quality jewelry images and descriptions in addition to the Images and descriptions the supplier offered them at no charge, improving their online store's visibility, value, and attractiveness. Many new repeat clients came on board.

4. Allocated more funds to marketing: The cost-saving benefits of dropshipping allowed Ocean Jewels to invest more in marketing efforts, driving increased website traffic and sales.

Measurable Outcomes:

1. Expanded Jewelry collections: Ocean Jewels was able to offer a broader selection of jewelry gifts to cater to diverse customer preferences, attracting a wider customer base and a higher end clientele.

2. Reduced overhead costs: By eliminating the need for inventory, tracking and restocking, the company experienced significant cost savings, improving their financial stability.

3. Improved order fulfillment: Leveraging suppliers' logistics capabilities enabled Ocean Jewels to process and ship customer orders more efficiently, enhancing customer satisfaction and loyalty.

4. Increased online visibility and sales: The enhanced online presence, coupled with effective digital marketing strategies, resulted in higher website traffic, brand awareness, and ultimately, increased sales.

Challenges Faced:

1. Supplier reliability: Ocean Jewels faced occasional challenges with suppliers, including delayed shipments or product quality issues, impacting customer satisfaction and the company's reputation, until they found the one that was proven and a long track record of reliability.

2. Striking a balance with inventory: With no inventory on hand, the company had to carefully manage supplier relationships to ensure a consistent supply of jewelry collections and timely order fulfillment.

Lessons Learned:

1. Establish strong supplier partnerships: Building relationships with a reliable supplier is crucial to ensure consistent product quality and timely order fulfillment.

2. Regularly review and analyze supplier performance: Regular assessments of supplier reliability and quality are vital to maintain customer satisfaction and the company's reputation.

3. Continuous marketing efforts are essential: While dropshipping provides many benefits, a proactive marketing strategy is essential to drive traffic and increase sales.

Overall Impact:

Ocean Jewels achieved significant growth and established themselves as a dominant player in the marketplace by incorporating dropshipping. Through an expanded jewelry range, reduced overhead costs, improved order fulfillment, and an enhanced online presence, they attracted more customers, increased sales, and improved their financial stability. The success of Ocean Jewels serves as a compelling case study for struggling dive, surf, ocean sports, and beach resort sea life jewelry giftshops considering dropshipping as an absolute game-changing strategy.

Now that we have examined the success of Ocean Jewels in transforming their beach resort jewelry giftshop through dropshipping, let's take a look at some of the key mistakes to avoid in implementing this strategy. By learning from these mistakes, struggling dive, surf, ocean sports beach resort sea life jewelry giftshops can effectively harness the benefits of dropshipping and avoid potential pitfalls.

Typical Mistakes And How To Avoid Them

Based on the material covered here, some common mistakes that people make in the area of dropshipping for retail jewelry gifts include:

1. Not partnering with a proven, reputable supplier: By building a close relationship for success allows for the supplier to give personal service and help their jewelry ranges expand and be the very best possible. They may not only cater to the diverse preferences of customers but now start to attract a new higher end customer base. There is huge value is building a strong relationship with a business dropship supplier that has the track record and resources.

2. Failing to reduce overhead costs: Holding inventory can be costly for businesses, especially if they have had it for some time or have to invest in large quantities of stock upfront. To avoid this mistake, businesses should consider dropshipping, which eliminates the need to hold inventory and helps improve cash flow.

3. Neglecting order fulfillment efficiency: Businesses that rely on their own storage and shipping infrastructure may experience delays in order processing and shipping. To avoid this, leveraging

the logistics capabilities of suppliers through dropshipping allows for a wider choice of collections and leads to faster and more efficient order fulfillment, improving customer satisfaction and loyalty.

4. Overlooking the importance of online presence: In today's digital age, having a strong online presence is crucial for businesses. Neglecting to enhance their online store with high-quality product images and descriptions, as well as effective digital marketing strategies, can limit brand awareness and website traffic. To avoid this mistake, businesses should collaborate with suppliers to showcase the beauty and uniqueness of each jewelry gift and invest in digital marketing efforts.

By avoiding these common mistakes and implementing dropshipping for retail jewelry gifts, businesses can expand their jewelry ranges, reduce costs, improve order fulfillment, and enhance their online presence to attract more customers, increase sales, and establish themselves in the market.

With these mistakes to avoid in mind, it is crucial to implement the #1 piece of advice: prioritize building strong partnerships with multiple reputable suppliers.

My #1 Piece Of Advice

The key advice for struggling dive, surf, ocean sports, and beach resort sea life jewelry gift shop owners and online store managers in the mid-level to high-end market is to focus on unique and beautifully crafted jewelry lines in both sterling silver and gold that truly capture the essence of the ocean and sea life, and will for sure grow your sales and business to the heights you've always dreamed of.

Summary:

- Expand your jewelry collections: By implementing dropshipping, you can offer a wider selection of jewelry gifts, catering to a broader range of customers with diverse tastes and preferences. Include bother fine sterling silver and gold jewelry collections to reach all buyers' wants and desires

- Reduce overhead costs: With dropshipping, you eliminate the need for large upfront investments in inventory, freeing up funds for marketing efforts and improving overall financial stability.
- Improve order fulfillment: Leveraging your suppliers' logistics capabilities enables faster processing and shipping, leading to increased customer satisfaction and loyalty.
- Enhance online presence: Collaborate with suppliers to create high-quality jewelry images and descriptions, coupled with well-executed digital marketing strategies, to increase brand awareness, website traffic, and ultimately, sales.
- Achieve success like Ocean Jewels: Follow in the footsteps of a successful jewelry giftshop by adopting dropshipping and positioning yourself as a dominant player in the market.

Quiz

Quiz Questions:

1. What business experienced tremendous growth after incorporating dropshipping into their business model?

2. What challenges did Ocean Jewels face before implementing dropshipping?

3. How did dropshipping allow Ocean Jewels to expand their product range?

4. What was one of the cost-saving benefits that Ocean Jewels gained from leveraging dropshipping?

5. How did dropshipping enable Ocean Jewels to fulfill customer orders more efficiently and promptly?

6. What did Ocean Jewels do to enhance their online presence and visibility?

7. How did Ocean Jewels attract more customers and increase sales?

8. What is the main benefit of adopting a dropshipping service for retail jewelry giftshops?

9. What type of businesses can benefit from implementing a dropshipping service?

10. What type of ocean-themed jewelry giftshop is used as an example in this material?

Answer Key:
1 - Ocean Jewels
2 - Limited stock availability, high inventory costs, and the inability to offer a wide selection of jewelry collections,
3 - By partnering with multiple reputable suppliers
4 - Improving their cash flow and overall financial stability
5 - By leveraging their suppliers' logistics capabilities
6 - Collaborated with their suppliers to create high-quality product images and descriptions
7 - By implementing well-executed digital marketing strategies
8 - To achieve significant results and establish themselves as a dominant player in the market
9- Retail jewelry giftshops
10 - Beach resort jewelry giftshop

Now that we've explored the impact of dropshipping in the retail jewelry gifts industry, let's dive deeper into another exciting avenue for businesses in the ocean sports, sea life, and nautical retail sector, where the addition of both Sterling Silver and 14, 18, and 22 Kt Gold products can bring immense benefits to their inventory. So, grab your snorkels and join us for an enlightening chapter ahead!

CHAPTER 3. BRING THE BRILLIANCE: UNLOCKING SUCCESS WITH PRECIOUS METALS IN SEA LIFE AND OCEAN SPORTS RETAIL

"Don't fall victim to stale inventory and overstock; embrace dropshipping to easily expand your product offerings and cater to diverse customer preferences."

- Discover how incorporating Sterling Silver and 14, 18, and 22 Kt Gold Jewelry Dropshipping can revolutionize your online store platform!
- Say goodbye to inventory hassles and hello to expanded product offerings with dropshipping!
- Increase your online presence and reach a global market with the help of reliable dropshippers.
- Lower costs, increase sales and dominate the ocean sports, sea life, and nautical jewelry market using dropshipping.
- Choose a reputable dropshipper to maintain your reputation and build customer trust.

Incorporating Sterling Silver and 14, 18, and 22 Kt Gold Jewelry Dropshipping in their online store platforms can provide numerous benefits for retail businesses selling ocean sports, sea life, and nautical jewelry gifts. By utilizing dropshipping, these businesses can significantly reduce their inventory levels and associated costs while expanding their product offerings and online presence.

First and foremost, dropshipping allows retailers to eliminate the need for stocking and managing large amounts of inventory. Instead of purchasing and storing jewelry items, the retailer can simply partner with a reliable dropshipper who will handle the inventory management and order fulfillment on behalf of the retailer. This eliminates the risk of overstocking or getting stuck with unsold inventory, which can lead to financial losses. By reducing inventory costs, retailers can allocate their resources to other aspects of their business, such as marketing or customer service.

Furthermore, incorporating dropshipping enables retailers to expand their product selection without the need to invest in additional inventory. Sterling Silver and 14, 18, and 22 Kt Gold jewelry are highly sought after by customers in the ocean sports, sea life, and nautical-themed market. By offering a wide range of jewelry options in these materials, retailers can cater to diverse customer preferences and increase their chances of making a sale. Dropshipping allows retailers to easily add new products to their online store without the risk of being left with stale inventory.

In addition to reducing inventory costs and expanding product offerings, dropshipping can also enhance a retailer's online presence and visibility. When retailers partner with dropshippers who offer worldwide delivery, they can tap into a global customer base. This opens up opportunities to reach customers in different geographical locations and expand their market reach. With the right marketing and promotion strategies, retailers can position themselves as key players in the online ocean sports, sea life, and nautical jewelry market.

It is essential to choose a dropshipper that is reliable, reputable, and efficient in order to ensure customer satisfaction. By partnering with a dropshipper that has a proven track record of delivering high-quality products and timely order fulfillment, retailers can maintain their reputation and build customer trust.

In conclusion, incorporating Sterling Silver and 14, 18, and 22 Kt Gold Jewelry Dropshipping in an online store platform can provide numerous benefits for retail businesses selling ocean sports, sea life, and nautical jewelry gifts. By reducing inventory costs, expanding product offerings, and improving online presence, retailers can increase sales, lower expenses, and dominate the market. However, it is crucial to carefully choose a reliable dropshipper that can deliver on promises and uphold the retailer's commitment to accuracy and quality.

Now that you have read about the benefits of incorporating Sterling Silver and 14, 18, and 22 Kt Gold Jewelry Dropshipping in an online store platform, it is important to have a checklist in place to choose a reliable dropshipper. This checklist will help ensure customer satisfaction and maintain your reputation as a retailer.

Checklist

How to Checklist for Incorporating Sterling Silver and Gold Jewelry Dropshipping:

1. Research and identify a reliable and reputable dropshipper in the jewelry industry that specializes in Sterling Silver and 14, 18, and 22 Kt Gold jewelry specifically for the ocean sports, sea life, and nautical-themed market.

2. Review the dropshipper's track record, including their experience, customer reviews, and order fulfillment history, to ensure they can deliver high-quality products and timely order fulfillment.

3. Contact the dropshipper and inquire about their services, including inventory management, order fulfillment, and shipping options. Discuss any specific requirements or preferences you have for your online store.

4. Negotiate pricing and terms with the dropshipper, ensuring that the profit margins are fair and competitive for your retail business.

5. Establish a partnership agreement with the dropshipper, outlining responsibilities, expectations, and policies regarding

inventory management, order fulfillment, returns, and customer service.

6. Set up your online store platform and integrate it with the dropshipper's inventory management system. Ensure that the product listings, prices, and availability are accurately reflected on your website.

7. Create compelling product descriptions and attractive visuals to showcase the Sterling Silver and Gold jewelry on your online store. Highlight the materials, designs, and unique features that appeal to your target customers.

8. Implement effective marketing and promotion strategies to increase your online presence and visibility in the ocean sports, sea life, and nautical jewelry market. Utilize various digital marketing channels such as social media, email marketing, and search engine optimization (SEO) to reach a wider audience.

9. Monitor and analyze your online store's performance, including sales, customer feedback, and website traffic. Make adjustments and improvements based on the data to optimize your dropshipping business.

10. Continuously communicate and collaborate with the dropshipper to address any issues, concerns, or changes in inventory, pricing, or shipping. Maintain a strong partnership to ensure customer satisfaction and long-term success.

11. Regularly review and update your product offerings based on market trends, customer preferences, and performance analysis. Continuously seek new and exciting Sterling Silver and Gold Jewelry options to keep your online store fresh and appealing to customers.

Remember, building a successful dropshipping business requires careful planning, diligent research, and strong communication and collaboration with your dropshipper. By following this checklist, you can maximize the benefits of dropshipping and establish a thriving online store selling ocean sports, sea life, and nautical jewelry gifts.

Now that we have gone through the checklist for incorporating Sterling Silver and Gold jewelry dropshipping, let's take a look at some examples that demonstrate how these steps can be applied in practice.

"Exercise caution when expanding your online presence; partner with a dropshipper who can deliver worldwide to tap into a global customer base."

Examples

Example 1: Sand Dollar is a retail business that specializes in selling ocean sports, sea life, and nautical jewelry gifts. By incorporating Sterling Silver and 14, 18, and 22 Kt Gold Jewelry Dropshipping in their online store platform, they can eliminate the need for stocking and managing large amounts of inventory. Instead, they partner with a reliable dropshipper who handles the inventory management and order fulfillment. This allows Company A to reduce inventory costs and allocate their resources to other aspects of their business, such as marketing or customer service.

Example 2: Manta Jewelry is a retail business that wants to expand their product offerings in the ocean sports, sea life, and nautical-themed market. By utilizing dropshipping, they can easily add Sterling Silver and 14, 18, and 22 Kt Gold jewelry to their online store without the need to invest in additional inventory. This allows Manta Jewelry to cater to diverse customer preferences and increase their chances of making a sale without the risk of being left with unsold inventory.

Example 3: SeaTurtle is a retail business that wants to expand their market reach and tap into a global customer base. By partnering with a dropshipper that offers worldwide delivery, they can reach customers in different geographical locations. This enhances their online presence and visibility, positioning them as key players in the online ocean sports, sea life, and nautical jewelry market.

Example 4: Black Tip Jewelry is a retail business that understands the importance of maintaining a good reputation and building customer trust. They carefully choose a reliable and reputable dropshipper with a proven track record of delivering high-quality, finely detailed jewelry and timely order fulfillment. By ensuring customer satisfaction, Company D can uphold their commitment to accuracy and quality, maintaining their reputation in the market.

Example 5: Company E is a retail business that wants to dominate the ocean sports, sea life, and nautical jewelry market. By incorporating Sterling Silver and 14, 18, and 22 Kt Gold Jewelry Dropshipping in their online store platform, they can increase sales and lower expenses. This allows Black Tip Jewelry to stay competitive and become a leader in the industry.

Based on these examples, it is clear that dropshipping can provide numerous advantages for retail businesses in the ocean sports, sea life, and nautical jewelry market. To further explore the benefits and potential of dropshipping in this industry, let's examine a detailed case study.

Case Study

Case Study: Ocean Treasures Jewelry - Reducing Inventory and Expanding Online Presence through Dropshipping

Introduction:
Ocean Treasures Jewelry is a retail business specializing in ocean sports, sea life, and nautical-themed jewelry gifts. The company aims to reduce inventory levels and implement a unique, business-expanding, reliable dropshipping service that delivers worldwide. This case study examines how Ocean Treasures

Jewelry successfully incorporated Sterling Silver and 14, 18, and 22 Kt Gold Jewelry Dropshipping to achieve their goals.

Key Aspects Covered:

1. Reducing Inventory Costs:

Ocean Treasures Jewelry partnered with a reliable dropshipper who handled inventory management and order fulfillment. By eliminating the need to purchase and store large amounts of inventory, the company significantly reduced costs associated with inventory management.

2. Expanding Jewelry Collections Offered:

Through dropshipping, Ocean Treasures Jewelry was able to expand its jewelry collections without the need to invest in additional inventory. The company started offering a wide range of jewelry options in Sterling Silver and 14, 18, and 22 Kt Gold, catering to diverse customer preferences and increasing chances of making a sale.

3. Enhancing Online Presence:

Ocean Treasures Jewelry partnered with a dropshipper offering worldwide delivery, allowing the company to tap into a global customer base. This enabled them to expand their market reach and enhance their online presence.

Specific Actions/Initiatives Implemented:

1. Research and Selection of Reliable Dropshipper:

Ocean Treasures Jewelry conducted thorough research to identify a dropshipper that could meet their requirements for reliability, reputation, and efficiency in order fulfillment. They chose a dropshipper with a proven track record of delivering high-quality Fine Jewelry with timely order fulfillment.

2. Product Catalog Expansion:

With the help of the dropshipper, Ocean Treasures Jewelry added a wide range of Sterling Silver and 14, 18, and 22 Kt Gold jewelry to their online store, offering customers a comprehensive selection of ocean sports, sea life, and nautical-themed jewelry gifts.

Measurable Outcomes Achieved:

1. Reduced Inventory Costs:

Ocean Treasures Jewelry saved significantly on inventory costs due to the elimination of the need for stocking and managing large amounts of inventory.

2. Increased Sales and Revenue:

The expansion of jewelry collection offerings and the company's enhanced online presence through dropshipping led to an increase in sales and revenue. Customers had a wider range of jewelry options available, leading to higher conversion rates.

Challenges Faced:

1. Finding a Reliable Dropshipper:

The most significant challenge Ocean Treasures Jewelry faced was finding a dropshipper that could deliver a wide range of both Sterling Silver and Gold Jewelry plus deliver on their promises and uphold the company's commitment to accuracy and quality. Thorough research and vetting were required to ensure the right partner was chosen.

Lessons Learned:

1. Partnering with a Reliable Dropshipper:

Ocean Treasures Jewelry learned the importance of partnering with a dropshipper that has a proven track record of delivering high-quality jewelry collections with great selections coupled with timely order fulfillment. A reliable dropshipper is crucial in maintaining the company's reputation and building customer trust.

Overall Assessment of Impact:

Ocean Treasures Jewelry's incorporation of Sterling Silver and 14, 18, and 22 Kt Gold Jewelry Dropshipping had a significant impact on their business. The company was able to reduce inventory costs, could expand jewelry design collections offered, enhance online presence, increase sales and revenue, and dominate the market in the ocean sports, sea life, and nautical-themed jewelry industry. By carefully selecting a reliable dropshipper, Ocean Treasures Jewelry successfully achieved their goals and experienced outstanding growth.

Now that we have examined how Ocean Treasures Jewelry successfully incorporated dropshipping to achieve their goals, let's take a closer look at some common mistakes to avoid when implementing a dropshipping strategy.

Typical Mistakes And How To Avoid Them

Most people make mistakes in dropshipping by not carefully choosing a reliable dropshipper. To avoid this, retailers must partner with a dropshipper that is reliable, reputable, communicates well and is efficient. This ensures customer satisfaction and helps maintain the retailer's reputation. Additionally, retailers should focus on reducing inventory costs, expanding with a variety of jewelry line offerings, and improving online presence to increase sales and lower expenses.

Now that we have discussed some common mistakes to avoid in dropshipping, let's move on to my #1 piece of advice that encompasses all of these factors.

> *"Ensure customer satisfaction and build trust by partnering with a dropshipper known for high-quality products and timely order fulfillment*

My #1 Piece Of Advice

Reduce inventory levels and implement a reliable dropshipping service for mid-level and high-end ocean sports, sea life, and nautical retail jewelry gifts. Build your business with proven sellers. Expand into new, higher end markets by adding gold and sterling silver jewelry to your online stores without the expense of an upfront inventory and get access to many new and unique sea life, water sports, nautical jewelry designs and collections. Up your game; up your customer base! Build repeat sales and watch your business expand and grow!

Summary:

- Reduce inventory costs while you increase profits: Incorporating dropshipping allows retailers to eliminate the need for stocking and managing large amounts of inventory, reducing the risk of overstocking and financial losses. This frees up resources to invest in other aspects of the business, such as marketing or customer service, ultimately boosting profitability.

- Expand Jewelry collections and cater to diverse customer preferences: With dropshipping, retailers can easily add a wide range of Sterling Silver and 14, 18, and 22 Kt Gold jewelry options to their online store, without the risk of being left with stagnant inventory. This allows them to attract and satisfy customers with different style preferences, increasing the chances of making a sale.

- Enhance online presence and reach global customers: Partnering with dropshippers that offer worldwide delivery enables retailers to tap into a global customer base. This expands their market reach and presents opportunities to position themselves as key players in the online ocean sports, sea life, and nautical jewelry market.

- Maintain reputation and build customer trust: Choosing a reliable and reputable dropshipper is crucial to ensure customer satisfaction. By partnering with a dropshipper with a proven track record of delivering high-quality products and timely order fulfillment, retailers can uphold their commitment of beauty, fine detail, and quality, maintaining their reputation and building trust among customers.

- Increase sales, lower expenses, and dominate the market: By incorporating Sterling Silver and 14, 18, and 22 Kt Gold Jewelry Dropshipping, retailers can experience a boost in sales, lower expenses through reduced inventory costs, and position themselves as leaders in the market. Taking action and embracing dropshipping can lead to significant growth and success in the ocean sports, sea life, and nautical jewelry industry.

Quiz

1. What are the benefits of partnering with a reliable dropshipper?
A. Reduced inventory costs
B. Expanded product selection
C. Enhanced online presence
D. All of the above

2. What type of jewelry materials are highly sought after by customers in the ocean sports, sea life, and nautical-themed market?
A. Sterling Silver
B. 14 Kt Gold
C. 18 Kt Gold
D. All of the above

3. What is the primary benefit of using dropshipping instead of stocking and managing inventory?
A. Increased customer satisfaction
B. Expanded product selection
C. Elimination of financial losses
D. Improved marketing strategies

4. What kind of risks can dropshipping help retailers avoid?
A. Overstocking
B. Poor customer service
C. Unsold inventory
D. Limited market reach

5. What type of strategies can retailers use to become key players

in the online ocean sports, sea life, and nautical jewelry market?
A. Investing in additional inventory
B. Partnering with a dropshipper
C. Developing marketing and promotion strategies
D. All of the above

6. What is the key to ensuring customer satisfaction when utilizing dropshipping?
A. Quality products
B. Timely order fulfillment
C. Global customer base
D. Reduced inventory costs

7. What is the primary advantage of dropshipping?
A. Increased customer satisfaction
B. Enhanced online presence
C. Elimination of inventory costs
D. Expanded product selection

8. What is the benefit of expanding product offerings with dropshipping?
A. Increased customer satisfaction
B. Lower expenses
C. Tap into a global customer base
D. Cater to diverse customer preferences

9. What can retailers do with resources freed up by reducing inventory costs?
A. Improve customer service
B. Expand their market reach
C. Stock more inventory
D. Increase marketing efforts

10. What should retailers consider when choosing a dropshipper?
A. Quality products
B. Reliability
C. Reputation
D. All of the above

Answer Key:

1. D. All of the above
2. D. All of the above
3. C. Elimination of financial losses
4. C. Unsold inventory
5. C. Developing marketing and promotion strategies
6. A. Quality products
7. C. Elimination of inventory costs
8. D. Cater to diverse customer preferences
9. A. Improve customer service
10. D. All of the above

"As we have explored in the previous chapter, incorporating Sterling Silver and various gold jewelry dropshipping options can greatly benefit retail businesses in the ocean sports, sea life, and nautical jewelry market. Now, let's take a closer look at some successful and targeted collections that have consistently proven to capture the hearts of customers in this specific niche, so keep reading to discover the secret behind their success!"

CHAPTER 4. DIVE INTO SUCCESS:
UNVEILING TARGETED COLLECTIONS
IN OCEAN SPORTS JEWELRY RETAIL

"The heart of man is very much like the sea; it has its storms, it has its tides, and in its depths, it has its pearls too." - Vincent Van Gogh

- Dive into the depths of the "Underwater Treasures Collection" and discover the exquisite beauty of marine-inspired jewelry.
- Hang ten with the "Surf's Up Collection" and let your love for the waves shine with beach-inspired jewelry pieces.
- Set sail with the "Nautical Luxuries Collection" and embrace the elegance of classic nautical-themed jewelry.
- Find your passion and make a statement with unique and high-quality ocean jewelry pieces.
- Discover how targeted collections are revolutionizing the market and driving sales in the ocean sports, sea life, and nautical retail jewelry industry.

Absolutely. In the ocean sports, sea life, and nautical retail jewelry market, there are several targeted collections that have proven to be highly successful in terms of increasing sales and dominating the market. These collections cater specifically to the interests and preferences of customers passionate about ocean sports, sea life, and nautical themes. Let me provide you with a few examples:

1. "Underwater Treasures Collection":
This collection features exquisite jewelry pieces inspired by the vibrant marine life found beneath the ocean's surface. It includes intricate designs of coral, seahorses, starfish, dolphins, and other

underwater creatures. The use of vibrant gemstones such as turquoise, aquamarine, and opal further enhances the beauty and allure of the collection. The "Underwater Treasures Collection" has resonated well with customers who seek unique and elegant jewelry that reflects their love for the sea.

2. "Surf SV Collection":

Designed specifically for surf enthusiasts, the "Surf's Up Collection" captures the essence of the sport and its connection to nature. This collection showcases jewelry pieces in the shape of surfboards, waves, and beach-inspired motifs. It incorporates elements like sterling silver and gold to add a touch of luxury. The "Surf's Up Collection" has appealed to customers who are passionate about surfing and want to wear jewelry that symbolizes their adventurous lifestyle.

3. "Nautical Luxuries Collection":

This collection is aimed at customers who appreciate the classic elegance of nautical-themed jewelry. It features timeless designs inspired by anchors, boats, compasses, and other maritime symbols. The use of high-quality materials like 14, 18, and 22 Kt gold adds a sense of luxury to the collection, making it highly desirable for those seeking high-end ocean jewelry pieces. The "Nautical Luxuries Collection" has proven to be particularly successful among customers who want to make a statement with their jewelry while embracing their love for the sea.

4. "The Expansive Sea Life Collection"

Our Collection of Fine Sterling Silver and Gold Sea Life jewelry is a true testament to the beauty and diversity of the marine world found in popular scuba dive resort locations worldwide. From the vibrant waters of Asia to the crystal-clear Caribbean and the mesmerizing Mediterranean, each piece in this stunning collection encapsulates the essence and allure of these magnificent destinations.

Immerse yourself in the enchanting world of the sea, where

delicate sea turtles gracefully glide through turquoise waters, elegant seahorses dance amidst vibrant coral reefs, and charming dolphins playfully leap in the spray. From the open waters of Thailand's whale sharks. Our talented artisans have meticulously crafted these exquisite sea creatures into intricate and breathtaking designs, capturing their essence in every shimmering detail.

Your customers will adorn themselves with your Fine Sterling Silver and Gold Sea Life jewelry, not only will you be showcasing your love for the ocean and its striking inhabitants, but you'll also be supporting sustainable and ethical practices. Each piece is crafted using responsibly sourced materials, ensuring the preservation of these delicate ecosystems for generations to come.

Whether you're an avid diver with a deep connection to the underwater world or simply someone who appreciates the beauty of sea life, our collection offers something for everyone. From elegant pendants and dainty earrings to statement rings and intricate bracelets, each piece is a wearable work of art that will spark conversation and evoke memories of your own unforgettable dive experiences.

Indulge your love for the sea and elevate your style with our Collection of Fine Sterling Silver and Gold Sea Life jewelry curated from scuba dive resort locations worldwide. Dive into the depths of beauty and let these exquisite pieces serve as a reminder of the awe-inspiring wonders that lie beneath the surface.

These examples demonstrate the success of targeted collections in the ocean sports, sea life, and nautical retail jewelry market. By offering a wide range of options that cater to the specific interests of customers, jewelry retailers have been able to increase sales, expand their online store presence, and lower inventory costs. Moreover, the popularity of such collections showcases the potential for dominating the market by delivering unique and high-quality jewelry selections.

Now that we have seen the success of targeted collections in the ocean sports, sea life, and nautical retail jewelry market, let's take a look at a checklist I have created to help you develop your own successful collection.

"To me, the sea is a continual miracle; the fishes that swim – the rocks – the motion of the waves – the ships, with men in them, what stranger miracles are there?" - Walt Whitman

Checklist

Decision-Making Checklist for Ocean Sports, Sea Life, and Nautical Retail Jewelry Market:

1. Identify the target market: Determine the specific customer base interested in ocean sports, sea life, and nautical themes. Consider their preferences, interests, and purchasing behaviors.

2. Research successful collections: Study existing collections that have proven to be highly successful in increasing sales and dominating the market. Analyze their designs, materials, and target audience appeal.

3. Design unique and exquisite jewelry pieces: Create jewelry pieces that reflect the interests and preferences of the target market. Incorporate intricate designs inspired by ocean life, surf culture, and nautical motifs.

4. Utilize vibrant gemstones and high-quality materials: Consider using gemstones that enhance the beauty and allure of the collection, such as sapphires, turquoise, aquamarine, and opal. Use high-quality materials like fine sterling silver and gold to add a touch of luxury to the jewelry pieces.

5. Ensure timeless and classic designs: Craft designs that showcase timeless elegance and capture the essence of ocean sports, sea life, and nautical themes. Incorporate symbols like Turtles, Manta Rays and Sharks.

6. Conduct market research and analysis: Conduct market research to understand customer preferences, buying trends, and competitors' offerings. Analyze market data to identify gaps and opportunities.

7. Consider online store presence: Develop a strong, expansive online presence to reach a wider audience and increase visibility. Create an engaging and user-friendly website or online store platform.

8. Manage Your Online Visible Inventory for Dropshipping: Optimize Cyber Inventory management to show more of the designs your viewers and buyers like and remove the design images that get no looks or attention. Monitor sales trends and adjust your online collections accordingly, giving you great leverage.

9. Integrate marketing and advertising strategies: Develop targeted marketing and advertising campaigns to promote the collections and reach the intended audience. Consider utilizing social media platforms, influencers, and collaborations.

10. Assess customer feedback and adapt: Monitor customer feedback and reviews to assess the success and relevance of collections. Use feedback to make improvements, introduce new designs, or expand the jewelry collections and lines.

11. Track sales performance and adjust strategies: Continuously monitor sales performance and identify areas of improvement. Adjust pricing, marketing strategies, or collection offerings based on sales data and customer feedback.

12. Maintain brand reputation: Deliver only high-quality, beautifully crafted jewelry with outstanding exceptional customer service to build and maintain a strong brand reputation. Aim for customer over-the-edge satisfaction and loyalty to drive repeat purchases.

By following this decision-making checklist, jewelry retailers can increase sales, dominate the market, and deliver unique and high-quality selections that resonate with customers passionate about ocean sports, sea life, and nautical themes.

"Let the sea set you free." - Unknown

Now that we have gone through the shopping checklist for ocean sports, sea life, and nautical retail jewelry, let's take a look at some examples that I have already prepared for each collection. Keep in mind that these are just a few examples, and you can expand the checklist based on your personal preferences and the available options within each collection.

Examples

1. "Mermaid Dreams Collection":
This collection is inspired by the mythical creature of mermaids and their enchanting underwater world. It features jewelry pieces adorned with shells, pearls, and mermaid tail designs. The use of delicate pastel colors and intricate details adds a whimsical touch to the collection, making it a favorite among customers who are captivated by the beauty and magic of mermaids.

2. "Seashell Elegance Collection":
Designed for customers who adore the natural beauty of seashells, the "Seashell Elegance Collection" offers a range of jewelry pieces crafted using real seashells. From delicate earrings to statement necklaces, the collection showcases the intricate patterns and textures of various seashells. By incorporating precious metal accents and gemstone embellishments, this collection allows customers to showcase their love for sea-inspired jewelry accessories in an elegant and sophisticated way.

3. "Sailor's Delight Collection":
This collection pays homage to the classic symbols associated with sailors and the sea. It includes jewelry pieces featuring

anchors, ship wheels, sailor knots, and compasses. The use of sterling silver, gold, and rope-inspired designs adds a touch of authenticity to the collection, making it a popular choice among customers who appreciate the timeless appeal of sailor-themed jewelry.

4. "Tropical Paradise Collection":
For customers who are drawn to the tropical vibes of beach resorts and island getaways, the "Tropical Paradise Collection" offers a range of vibrant and colorful jewelry pieces. Inspired by the flora and fauna found in tropical locations, this collection showcases jewelry adorned with palm trees, hibiscus flowers, pineapples, and other exotic motifs. The use of bright gemstones, enamel, and playful designs adds a sense of fun and relaxation, perfect for those who want to bring a piece of the tropics with them wherever they go.

These examples are just a few that illustrate how targeted collections in the ocean sports, sea life, and nautical retail jewelry market cater to a wide range of interests and preferences. By creating jewelry that resonates with customers' passions, retailers can successfully capture their attention, increase sales, and establish themselves as dominant players in the market.

> *"The sea is both beautiful and dangerous,*
> *and so is love." – Unknown*

Now, let's take a closer look at a case study that showcases how targeted collections in the ocean sports, sea life, and nautical retail jewelry market can effectively capture customers' attention and increase sales.

Case Study

Case Study: Ocean Jewelry Co. - Dominating the Market with Targeted Collections

Introduction:

Ocean Jewelry Co. is a retailer specializing in ocean sports, sea life, and nautical-themed jewelry. In order to reduce inventory levels and expand their business, they implemented a unique dropshipping service that delivers worldwide. To maximize their impact, they focused on creating targeted collections that catered to the specific interests and preferences of their customers.

Key Actions and Initiatives:
1. Creation of the "Underwater Treasures Collection":
Ocean Jewelry Co. developed a collection inspired by the vibrant marine life found beneath the ocean's surface. They incorporated intricate designs of coral, seahorses, starfish, dolphins, and other underwater creatures, using vibrant gemstones such as turquoise, aquamarine, and opal to enhance their beauty. This collection aimed to attract customers seeking unique and elegant jewelry that reflected their love for the sea.

2. Development of the "Surf SV Collection":
To cater to surf enthusiasts, Ocean Jewelry Co. put together a collection that captured the essence of the sport and its connection to nature. The collection featured jewelry pieces in the shape of surfboards, waves, flowers and beach-inspired motifs. By incorporating elements like sterling silver and gold, they added a touch of luxury. This collection aimed to appeal to customers passionate about surfing and looking for jewelry that symbolized their adventurous lifestyle.

3. Introduction of the "Nautical Luxuries Collection":
Ocean Jewelry Co. targeted customers who appreciated the classic elegance of nautical-themed jewelry with this collection. They selected timeless designs inspired by anchors, boats ship's wheels, compasses, and other maritime symbols of the Sea, using the high-quality precious metals of a split offering of both Sterling Silver and 14, 18, and 22 Kt gold to add a sense of luxury understanding all are treasures of the Sea. The "Nautical Luxuries Collection" aimed to appeal to customers who wanted to make a statement with their jewelry while embracing their love for the

sea.

Measurable Outcomes:

1. Increased Sales: The introduction of targeted collections resulted in a significant increase in sales for Ocean Jewelry Co. Customers were drawn to the unique designs and craftsmanship of the jewelry pieces, leading to a higher conversion rate and average order value.

2. Global Expansion: The implementation of a reliable dropshipping service enabled Ocean Jewelry Co. to deliver their collections worldwide. This expansion helped them reach a broader customer base and increase their market share in the ocean sports, sea life, and nautical retail jewelry industry.

3. Lower Inventory Levels and Costs: By focusing on targeted collections, Ocean Jewelry Co. could better manage their inventory levels and reduce costs. As they developed a deep understanding of their customers' preferences, they only produced items that were in high demand, minimizing the risk of excess stock.

Challenges Faced:

1. Design Consistency: Ensuring consistent design aesthetics across different collections was a challenge for Ocean Jewelry Co. to initially find. They needed to maintain a coherent brand identity while catering to various customer interests and preferences.

2. Global Shipping Logistics: Implementing a reliable dropshipping service that could deliver worldwide required careful coordination form the dropshipper. Overcoming logistical challenges and ensuring timely delivery were essential for customer satisfaction.

Lessons Learned:

1. Customer-Centric Approach: The success of Ocean Jewelry Co.'s targeted collections highlighted the importance of understanding

and catering to customers' specific interests and preferences. By focusing on their passions, the company was able to choose and market a variety of collections of jewelry that resonated strongly with their target market because they embraced the power that dropshipping gave them the many hundreds of unique designs and collections offered, to select from.

2. Collaboration and Partnerships: Building a strong partnership with long-term successful proven dropshipper removed all challenges for both domestic and international shipping as the dropship partner handled all seamlessly and successfully for them. This service included ensured the success of Ocean Jewelry Co.'s global expansion and dropshipping service. Collaboration helped them overcome any perceived logistical challenges and enhanced their customer experience.

Overall Assessment:
Ocean Jewelry Co.'s strategic focus on targeted collections and the implementation of a reliable dropshipping service have had a significant impact on their business. They have successfully reduced inventory levels and costs while increasing sales and global market presence. By understanding their customers and delivering unique and high-quality jewelry selections, they have positioned themselves as a dominant player in the ocean sports, sea life, and nautical retail jewelry industry.

Now that we have examined Ocean Jewelry Co.'s successful initiatives and measurable outcomes, let's take a look at some crucial mistakes to avoid to ensure continued success in dominating the market with targeted collections.

Typical Mistakes And How To Avoid Them

One mistake that most people make in the ocean sports, sea life, and nautical retail jewelry market is not targeting their collections specifically to the interests and preferences of customers. They overlook the dropshipper best-selling list made available targeting various markets throughout the world. To avoid this mistake, retailers should create collections that reflect their passion and love for the sea, such as the "Underwater Treasures Collection," "Surf's SV Collection," "Nautical Luxuries Collection" and "The Sea Life Collection" mentioned in the material coupled with the existing best sellers list. These collections have proven to be highly successful because they cater to the specific interests of customers and offer unique and elegant jewelry pieces. Another mistake people make is not using high-quality dropship companies for their nautical-themed jewelry. Finding a successful long-term dropshipper with a proven track record with both consistently fine quality sterling silver and gold jewelry solved their challenge.

Now that we have discussed the common mistakes to avoid in the ocean sports, sea life, and nautical retail jewelry market, let's dive into the #1 piece of advice that can help retailers overcome these challenges and achieve great success.

My #1 Piece Of Advice

My #1 piece of advice for struggling dive, surf, ocean sports, and resort sea life jewelry online stores is to reduce inventory levels and implement a unique, business-expanding, reliable Sterling Silver and 14, 18 and 22 Kt Gold Dropshipping service delivering to their customers worldwide for mid-level and high-end finely crafted precious metals jewelry. This growth model has shown outstanding results and can help boost your business in very big ways. Action is the Key!

Summary:

- Discover the breathtaking beauty of the "Underwater Treasures Collection" and experience the allure of vibrant marine life in stunning jewelry designs.
- Ride the wave of adventure with the "Surf SV Collection" and wear jewelry that truly represents your passion for

the surf and the natural world.

- Set sail with elegance and sophistication by embracing the timeless designs of the "Nautical Luxuries Collection" and make a statement with high-end ocean-themed jewelry.
- Take a leap into the ocean sports, sea life, and nautical retail jewelry market and tap into the immense potential for success and increased sales.
- Stand out from the competition by offering uniquely targeted collections that cater to the specific interests, passions and preferences of your customers, and become a dominant force in the industry.

Quiz

1. Is it possible to increase sales and dominate the market in the ocean sports, sea life, and nautical retail jewelry market?

2. What collection features intricate designs of coral, seahorses, starfish, dolphins, and other underwater creatures?

3. What collection is designed specifically for surf enthusiasts?

4. What collection is aimed at customers who appreciate the classic elegance of nautical-themed jewelry?

5. What materials are used in the "Nautical Luxuries Collection" to add a sense of luxury?

6. What are the benefits of targeted collections for jewelry retailers?

7. What element enhances the beauty and allure of the "Underwater Treasures Collection"?

8. What kind of statement do customers want to make with jewelry from the "Nautical Luxuries Collection"?

9. What does the "Surf's Up Collection" incorporate to add a touch of luxury?

10. What has been the success of targeted collections in the ocean sports, sea life, and nautical retail jewelry market?

***

Answer Key:

1. Absolutely
2. Underwater Treasures Collection
3. Surf's Up Collection
4. Nautical Luxuries Collection
5. 14, 18, and 22 Kt gold
6. Increase sales, expand their online store presence, and lower inventory costs
7. Gemstones such as turquoise, aquamarine, and opal
8. Make a statement
9. Sterling silver and gold
10. Highly successful

As we explore the success stories of targeted collections in the ocean sports, sea life, and nautical retail jewelry market, it is crucial to understand the key factors that ensure the reliability and quality of Dropshipping products, and how businesses can create a seamless experience for their customers – so keep reading and discover the secrets behind a thriving jewelry business!

CHAPTER 5. ANCHORING QUALITY: ENSURING RELIABILITY AND EXCELLENCE IN DROPSHIPPING JEWELRY

"Quality is never an accident; it is always the result of high intention, sincere effort, intelligent direction and skillful execution." - William A. Foster

- Discover the secrets to thriving in the ocean sports, sea life, and nautical retail jewelry market.
- Uncover the steps to ensuring the reliability, quality, and beauty of your Dropship jewelry.
- Learn how to choose a reputable supplier and select exclusive designs in fine sterling silver and gold that will bring more sales.
- Find out how to maintain open lines of communication and build strong relationships to guarantee success.
- Get insider tips on implementing a rigorous quality control system and offering guarantees and warranties to maintain customer satisfaction.

Answer: Ensuring the reliability, quality, and beauty of Dropshipping jewelry is crucial for businesses looking to thrive in the ocean sports, sea life, and nautical retail jewelry market. Here are some key steps businesses can take to achieve this:

1. Partner with reputable suppliers: The first step is to carefully vet and select trustworthy suppliers who specialize in creating exclusive designed jewelry in fine sterling silver and gold. Look for suppliers with a strong track record of delivering high-quality products and providing excellent customer service.

2. Thoroughly evaluate product samples: Before finalizing any partnership, request samples of the jewelry you plan to sell.

Examine these samples closely to check for craftsmanship, durability, and overall aesthetic appeal. Ensure that the finished products match your expectations and meet the quality standards you want to uphold.

3. Maintain open lines of communication: Building a strong relationship with your supplier is crucial for maintaining reliability and quality. Regularly communicate your expectations, providing detailed specifications and ensuring they are understood. Establish a feedback loop to address any concerns or issues promptly.

4. Conduct regular quality inspections: Implement a rigorous quality control system to ensure that every piece of jewelry that passes through your business meets your high standards. Consider partnering with an independent third-party inspection company to conduct random checks on the jewelry. This will provide an extra level of assurance and peace of mind for your customers.

5. Offer guarantees and warranties: Assure your customers of the reliability and quality of your Dropshipping jewelry by providing guarantees and warranties. Clearly communicate these policies to instill confidence in your products. Stand behind your jewelry, and if any issues arise, promptly address them to maintain customer satisfaction.

By following these steps, businesses can be confident that they are offering reliable, high-quality, and beautiful jewelry through their Dropshipping service. Building strong relationships with reputable suppliers, conducting quality inspections, and providing guarantees are crucial factors in establishing your brand as a trusted leader in the market.

Transition statement: Now that we have explored the key steps that businesses can take to ensure the reliability, quality, and beauty of Dropshipping jewelry, let's dive into the checklist that can help you implement these strategies effectively.

"Quality is more important than quantity.
One home run is much better than two doubles." - Steve Jobs

Checklist

Checklist for Ensuring the Reliability, Quality, and Beauty of Dropshipping Jewelry:

1. Research and select reputable suppliers specializing in fine sterling silver and gold jewelry.
2. Request product samples to evaluate craftsmanship, durability, and overall aesthetic appeal.
3. Maintain open lines of communication with suppliers to set clear expectations and provide detailed specifications.
4. Establish a feedback loop to address any concerns or issues promptly.
5. Implement a rigorous quality control system to inspect every piece of jewelry for quality assurance.
6. Consider partnering with an independent third-party inspection company for random checks.
7. Offer guarantees and warranties to assure customers of the reliability and quality of your jewelry.
8. Clearly communicate these policies to instill confidence in your products.
9. Stand behind your jewelry and promptly address any issues that may arise.
10. Build strong relationships with suppliers to establish your brand as a trusted leader in the market.

Now that we have gone through the checklist for ensuring the reliability, quality, and beauty of dropshipping jewelry, let's take a look at the examples I have prepared to illustrate these points.

Examples

Example 1: A business in the ocean sports industry looking to sell nautical-themed jewelry partners with a reputable supplier that has years of experience creating exclusive designs in fine sterling silver and gold. They carefully vet the supplier's track record and customer feedback, ensuring that they have a reputation for consistently delivering high-quality products.

Example 2: Before finalizing their partnership, the business requests samples of the jewelry they plan to sell. They closely examine the samples, checking for craftsmanship, durability, and overall aesthetic appeal. If the finished products do not meet their expectations or quality standards, they continue their search for a supplier who can provide the desired level of reliability and quality.

Example 3: The business maintains open lines of communication with their supplier. They regularly communicate their expectations, providing detailed specifications and ensuring they are understood. This allows for a collaborative relationship in which the supplier can offer suggestions and insights to improve the overall quality of the jewelry.

Example 4: To further ensure quality, the business implements a rigorous quality control system. They conduct regular inspections of every piece of jewelry that passes through their business, checking for any defects or issues. They also choose to partner with an independent third-party inspection company to conduct random checks on the jewelry. This adds an extra level of assurance and ensures that their customers can trust in the reliability and quality of the jewelry.

Example 5: To instill confidence in their customers, the business offers guarantees and warranties for their Dropshipping jewelry. They clearly communicate these policies, assuring customers that if any issues arise, they will promptly address them to maintain customer satisfaction. This commitment to standing behind their jewelry helps build trust and loyalty among their customer bases.

"In the end, we only regret the chances we didn't take." - Lewis Carroll

Based on these examples, I would like to present a case study that showcases how a business in the ocean sports industry successfully built a reliable and high-quality supply chain for their nautical-themed jewelry.

Case Study

Case Study: Ocean Treasures Jewelry Co.

Ocean Treasures Jewelry Co. is a mid-level and high-end ocean sports, sea life, and nautical retail jewelry company that specializes in delivering exclusive designed jewelry in fine sterling silver and gold worldwide through a successful Dropshipping service. This case study examines the key aspects discussed in the article and highlights the initiatives implemented, measurable outcomes achieved, challenges faced, lessons learned, and the overall impact on the company.

Initiatives Implemented:
1. Partnering with reputable suppliers: Ocean Treasures Jewelry Co. carefully selected reputable suppliers with a strong track record in creating high-quality jewelry. These suppliers specialized in designing exclusive pieces in fine sterling silver and gold that aligned with the company's brand.

2. Thorough evaluation of product samples: As part of the supplier selection process, Ocean Treasures Jewelry Co. requested samples of the jewelry they planned to sell. The company examined these samples closely to ensure craftsmanship, durability, and overall aesthetic appeal. Only suppliers whose products met the company's quality standards were considered for partnership.

3. Communication and feedback loop: Ocean Treasures Jewelry Co. established open lines of communication with their suppliers, regularly communicating their expectations and providing detailed specifications. They ensured that all parties involved understood the quality standards and design requirements. A

feedback loop was established to address any concerns or issues promptly and effectively.

4. Regular quality inspections: Ocean Treasures Jewelry Co. implemented a rigorous quality control system, conducting regular inspections to ensure that every piece of jewelry met their high standards. They partnered with an independent third-party inspection company to conduct random checks, further assuring the quality and reliability of their products.

5. Offering guarantees and warranties: To instill confidence in their products, Ocean Treasures Jewelry Co. offered guarantees and warranties to their customers. They clearly communicated these policies, assuring buyers of the reliability and quality of their Dropshipping jewelry. In cases where issues arose, the company promptly addressed them to maintain customer satisfaction.

Measurable Outcomes:
1. Increased customer satisfaction: By prioritizing reliability and quality, Ocean Treasures Jewelry Co. saw an increase in customer satisfaction. Positive customer reviews and feedback indicated that the company successfully delivered beautifully designed jewelry that met or exceeded expectations.

2. Enhanced reputation: Ocean Treasures Jewelry Co. established itself as a trusted leader in the ocean sports, sea life, and nautical retail jewelry market. Customers recognized the company's commitment to delivering high-quality products through their Dropshipping service, leading to an improved reputation and increased brand value.

Challenges Faced:
1. Supplier selection: Finding reputable suppliers that specialized in creating exclusive designed jewelry in fine sterling silver and gold was a challenge. It required thorough research, vetting, and careful evaluation to ensure a partnership with reliable suppliers.

2. Quality control: Maintaining consistent quality across a wide range of products proved to be a challenge. Regular quality inspections and addressing any issues promptly helped overcome this challenge.

Lessons Learned:
1. Building strong relationships with suppliers is crucial for maintaining reliability and quality. Effective communication and a feedback loop facilitated a collaborative partnership.

2. Regular quality inspections and involving independent third-party inspection companies added an extra layer of assurance and improved customer confidence.

Overall Assessment:
Ocean Treasures Jewelry Co. successfully implemented key initiatives to ensure the reliability, quality, and beauty of their Dropshipping jewelry. By partnering with reputable suppliers, conducting thorough evaluations, maintaining open lines of communication, conducting regular quality inspections, and offering guarantees and warranties, the company achieved increased customer satisfaction and an enhanced reputation. Ocean Treasures Jewelry Co. is now recognized as a trusted leader in the ocean sports, sea life, and nautical retail jewelry market, delivering high-quality products worldwide.

> *"The biggest risk is not taking any risk. In a world that's changing so quickly, the only strategy that is guaranteed to fail is not taking risks." - Mark Zuckerberg*

Now that we have examined the successful initiatives, measurable outcomes, challenges faced, and lessons learned by Ocean Treasures Jewelry Co., it is important to also consider the mistakes to avoid in this process. By understanding the potential pitfalls, other businesses can ensure a smoother implementation of similar strategies and avoid unnecessary setbacks.

Typical Mistakes And How To Avoid Them

Most people make the mistake of not thoroughly vetting suppliers. This can be avoided by carefully evaluating the track record and customer service of potential suppliers. Additionally, people often fail to conduct quality inspections. This can be avoided by implementing a rigorous quality control system and partnering with a third-party inspection company. Finally, many people neglect to offer guarantees and warranties. This can be avoided by clearly communicating these policies to instill confidence in customers.

Now that we have discussed the mistakes to avoid when it comes to vetting suppliers, conducting quality inspections, and offering guarantees and warranties, it is crucial to focus on the #1 piece of advice to prevent these common pitfalls.

My #1 Piece Of Advice

My #1 piece of advice for owners, operators, and managers of struggling dive, surf, ocean sports, and beach resort sea life jewelry gift shops with an online store would be to explore utilizing a Dropshipping service. There are companies that offer excellent quality, exclusive designed jewelry in fine sterling silver and gold, with the ability to deliver worldwide. This can greatly expand your product range and attract mid-level and high-end customers interested in ocean sports, sea life, and nautical retail jewelry gifts.

Summary:

- Partner with reputable suppliers who specialize in exclusive designed jewelry in fine sterling silver and gold.
- Thoroughly evaluate product samples for craftsmanship, durability, and aesthetic appeal.

- Maintain open lines of communication with suppliers to ensure reliability and quality.
- Conduct regular quality inspections to uphold high standards.
- Offer guarantees and warranties to instill confidence and maintain customer satisfaction.

Quiz

Questions:

1. What are some key steps businesses can take to ensure the reliability, quality, and beauty of Dropshipping jewelry?
A. Vet and select trustworthy suppliers
B. Evaluate product samples
C. Maintain open lines of communication
D. Conduct regular quality inspections
E. Offer guarantees and warranties

2. What should businesses consider when selecting a supplier for Dropshipping jewelry?
A. Price
B. Track record of delivering high-quality products
C. Experience in the jewelry industry
D. Variety of products offered
E. Location

3. What should businesses do to ensure that the finished products meet their expectations?
A. Request samples
B. Examine the samples closely
C. Establish a feedback loop
D. Offer guarantees and warranties
E. Conduct regular quality inspections

4. What is a crucial factor in establishing a brand as a trusted leader in the jewelry market?
A. Providing guarantees and warranties

B. Building strong relationships with suppliers
C. Offering a wide variety of products
D. Advertising the jewelry
E. Lowering prices

5. What should businesses do if any issues arise with their Dropshipping jewelry?
A. Ignore the issue
B. Offer a discount
C. Promote the jewelry
D. Promptly address the issue
E. Return the jewelry

6. What is an important step to take when examining jewelry samples?
A. Check for craftsmanship
B. Test for durability
C. Inspect the packaging
D. Calculate the price
E. Analyze the design

7. How can businesses provide assurance to customers that their Dropshipping jewelry is reliable and of high quality?
A. Offer discounts
B. Provide guarantees and warranties
C. Offer returns and refunds
D. Conduct regular quality inspections
E. Implement a feedback system

8. What should businesses consider implementing to provide an extra level of assurance for their customers?
A. A feedback system
B. Random checks
C. Advertising campaigns
D. A third-party inspection company
E. A customer loyalty program

9. What is the first step businesses should take when looking to

partner with a supplier for Dropshipping jewelry?
A. Request samples
B. Vet and select trustworthy suppliers
C. Carefully examine the jewelry
D. Offer guarantees and warranties
E. Establish open lines of communication

10. What should businesses do to maintain customer satisfaction?
A. Offer discounts
B. Lower prices
C. Ignore customer concerns
D. Promote the jewelry
E. Promptly address any issues

Answer Key:
1. A, B, C, D, E
2. B, C, D, E
3. A, B, C, D, E
4. A, B, C
5. D, E
6. A, B, C, E
7. A, B, D, E
8. D, E
9. B
10. D, E

Now that we have explored the general aspects of ensuring reliability and quality in Dropshipping jewelry, it's equally crucial to examine the specific complexities and challenges that arise when dealing with higher-end jewelry designs like 18 and 22 Kt Gold jewelry – let's dig deeper into this fascinating world and unravel the secrets behind its splendor!

CHAPTER 6. TRACKING DROPSHIPPING TRIUMPH: ESSENTIAL METRICS FOR DROPSHIP VIRTUAL INVENTORY MANAGEMENT SUCCESS

"Customer feedback: The GPS of dropshipping, pointing you in the right direction for improvement."

- Unlock the secrets of dropshipping success with invaluable insights from specific metrics and data points.
- Discover the top-selling designs and understand customer demand patterns to maximize profitability.
- Improve your jewelry collection performance and increase revenue by analyzing conversion rates and click-through rates.
- Harness the power of customer feedback to refine your dropship inventory management strategies and ensure customer satisfaction.
- Optimize your inventory interests, reduce wasted online real estate by identifying slow-moving and little-viewed items, and capitalize on high-demand, high-view jewelry designs and collections.

In the world of dropshipping, it is crucial for businesses to monitor specific metrics and data points to track the success of their dropship inventory management strategies. By doing so, owners, operators, and managers of online stores can gain valuable insights into what is selling well and what is not, allowing them to make informed decisions about expanding or contracting their virtual inventory.

First and foremost, businesses should closely track sales data. Tracking includes monitoring the overall sales volume, as well as sales performance or individual jewelry designs. By analyzing sales data, businesses can identify their best-selling items and understand the demand patterns of their customer base. This enables them to focus on promoting the jewelry that is most popular and profitable.

In addition to sales data, businesses should also monitor jewelry collection performance metrics. These metrics provide insights into how well a specific design or collection is performing in terms of conversion rates, click-through rates, and average order value. By analyzing this data, businesses can identify products that have high conversion rates and bring in significant revenue, as well as jewelry that may need to be improved or removed from their online store collections.

Furthermore, businesses should pay attention to customer feedback and reviews. By monitoring customer reviews and feedback, businesses can gauge customer satisfaction and identify any areas for improvement. The monitoring could involve adjusting jewelry descriptions, enhancing jewelry image quality, or addressing any issues that customers may have encountered. Customer feedback is a valuable source of information that can help businesses refine their dropship inventory management strategies and ensure customer satisfaction.

When an online store implements Dropshipping, the scenario below is no longer a concern or issue and resolves cash flow and costly time wasted:
This inventory turnover would be an essential metric to monitor IF and only if you did not implement a Dropship system.

* *This metric calculates how quickly on-hand inventory is being sold and replenished. By tracking inventory turnover, businesses can identify slow-moving items that may tie up capital and occupy <u>valuable shelf space</u>. They can then make data-driven decisions to reduce inventory costs by eliminating or reducing the quantity of these items. On the other hand, high turnover rates for certain products can*

indicate strong demand, prompting businesses to consider expanding their inventory for those items. – This <u>entire ongoing process</u> is all very costly, ties up cash flow and wastes valuable time and costs in lost sales.

The above* metric goes away when a store implements a Dropshipping System with inherent inventory management automation and reporting. Your life and business significantly change.

Lastly, businesses should analyze website traffic and visitor behavior metrics. By monitoring metrics such as the number of unique visitors, time spent on site, bounce rate, and conversion rate, businesses can gain insights into how well their online store is performing. This data can help them identify areas for improvement, such as optimizing jewelry placement, enhancing the user experience, or investing in targeted marketing campaigns to attract more visitors and increase conversions.

Overall, businesses should establish a comprehensive approach to monitoring and analyzing dropship inventory metrics and data points. By closely tracking sales data, Jewelry collection performance, customer feedback, inventory interest, and website traffic metrics, businesses can make data-driven decisions to optimize their dropship virtual inventory management strategies, increase their sales, and effectively grow their customer base.

Now that we have explored the importance of monitoring dropship inventory metrics and data points, it is time to delve into our checklist. This checklist includes key steps and considerations for businesses as they track sales data, monitor jewelry design performance, analyze customer feedback, track inventory interest, and evaluate website traffic. By following this checklist, businesses can make informed decisions and optimize their dropship online virtual inventory management strategies.

"Dropship Inventory management: Where slow-

moving items meet their match
- the delete button."

Checklist

How to Checklist for Monitoring Dropship Virtual Inventory Metrics:

1. Track sales data:
- Monitor overall sales volume
- Analyze sales performance for individual designs and collections
- Identify best-selling items and understand demand patterns

2. Monitor Jewelry trend performance metrics:
- Track conversion rates, click-through rates, and average order value
- Identify jewelry designs with high conversion rates and significant revenue
- Evaluate designs that may need image improvement or removal from inventory

3. Pay attention to customer feedback and reviews:
- Monitor customer satisfaction and identify areas for improvement
- Adjust Jewelry descriptions or enhance Image quality as needed
- Address any issues customers may have encountered

4. Track inventory sales:
- Calculate how quickly online designs are being sold
- Identify slow-moving items that may be tying up online space in your store.
- Make data-driven decisions to manage inventory shown or marketed online

5. Analyze website traffic and visitor behavior metrics:
- Monitor the number of unique visitors, time spent on site, bounce rate, and conversion rates
- Identify areas for improvement in jewelry placement or user experience

- Invest in targeted marketing campaigns to attract more visitors and increase conversions

6. Establish a comprehensive approach to monitoring and analyzing metrics:
- Regularly track and analyze sales data, jewelry design performance, customer feedback, virtual inventory sales, and website traffic metrics
- Make data-driven decisions to optimize dropship inventory image and marketing management strategies and increase sales
- Continuously grow and improve the customer base by using insights gained from monitoring metrics.

Now that we have gone through this checklist for monitoring dropship virtual inventory metrics, let's take a look at some examples that illustrate how each of these steps can be applied in practice.

Examples

Sales data: A dropshipping business notices that its overall sales volume has increased significantly over the past month. Upon further analysis, they find that their best-selling items are their shark jewelry collections, particularly Hammerhead Sharks. Armed with this information, they can now focus on promoting and showing different types and species of shark jewelry designs to capitalize on their success.

Jewelry collection performance metrics: An online store specializing in gold sea life jewelry notices that a specific manta ray design in their online inventory has a high conversion rate, with a large percentage of customers who view the product ultimately making a purchase. This data indicates that this pendant design is in high demand and brings in significant revenue, prompting the business to consider expanding their inventory with new manta ray earring, ring and bracelet designs similar to this item that will now encourage the buyers to purchase an entire gold manta ray set, substantially increasing sales in this collection.

Inventory turnover: A dropshipping business notices that a particular collection of tropical fish jewelry designs has been promoted in their online inventory for an extended period without being sold. By checking their online stats regularly, they realize that this jewelry collection of tropical fish has a slow turnover rate, tying up valuable visual online store space. With this information, the business can decide to reduce the quantity or eliminate this collection from their store and marketing campaigns and start showing a different, new sea life collection of seahorse jewelry or other collections they have in line to present and test.

Website traffic and visitor behavior metrics: An online store that has a specialty collection of Scuba diving-related jewelry designs. They notice a high bounce rate and short average time spent on these designs. By analyzing the metrics, they discovered that the jewelry pages for the dive jewelry designs are not effectively engaging visitors. Armed with this information, they can optimize the placement and presentation of these designs, enhance the user experience, and invest time in targeted marketing campaigns to attract more scuba-focused visitors and increase conversions by focusing in on SEO, Keywords and hashtags.

Now that we have explored these examples of data analysis in various aspects of an e-commerce business, let us delve into a case study that showcases how a dropshipping business utilizes data insights to make informed decisions and drive success.

Case Study

Case Study: Enhancing Dropship Virtual Inventory Management Strategies through Data Analysis

Introduction:

Dive-X is an online retailer that specializes in dropshipping. To improve their inventory management strategies and optimize sales, they decided to implement a comprehensive approach to monitor and analyze different metrics and data points.

Key Actions and Initiatives:

1. Sales Data Analysis:

Dive-X closely tracked their sales volume and individual jewelry design performance. By analyzing sales data, they were able to identify their best-selling items and understand demand patterns. This analysis allowed them to focus on promoting and stocking popular and profitable collections.

2. Jewelry Collection Performance Metrics:

The company monitored each design's conversion rates, click-through rates, and average order value. They analyzed this data to identify the jewelry with high conversion rates that brought significant revenue. They also identified designs that needed improvement or removal from their inventory.

3. Customer Feedback and Reviews:

By monitoring customer reviews and feedback, Dive-X gauged customer satisfaction and identified areas for improvement. They utilized this information to refine their dropship inventory management strategies, including adjusting jewelry design descriptions, improving jewelry image quality, and addressing customer comments and feedback.

4. Inventory Turnover Analysis:

Dive-X tracked inventory interest and sales to identify slow-moving items that were tying up online premium jewelry image space. With this data, they made data-driven decisions to replace images immediately by simply deleting the images they wanted out and replacing them with a jewelry collection closely related to another good selling range they wanted to put out and start testing. High purchase rates for specific designs indicated strong demand and prompted the business to expand inventory for those items.

5. Website Traffic and Visitor Behavior Metrics:
The company monitored metrics like the number of unique visitors, time spent on site, bounce rate, and conversion rate. This data provided insights into the performance of their online store. It helped identify areas for improvement, optimize jewelry design collection placement, enhance the user experience, and invest in targeted marketing campaigns to attract more visitors and increase conversions.

Measurable Outcomes:
1. Increased Sales: Dive-X experienced a 15% increase in sales within six months by focusing on their best-selling designs and responding to customer feedback.

2. Cost Reduction: By eliminating slow-moving items from their inventory, they reduced virtual inventory space waste by 18% and freed up premium space exposure.

3. Improved Customer Satisfaction: By addressing customer issues and enhancing product quality, Dive-X saw an increase in positive reviews and customer satisfaction improved by 21%.

Challenges Faced:
1. Data Analysis: Dive-X faced challenges in collecting and analyzing large amounts of data. They invested in software and training to streamline the process.

2. Jewelry Collection Improvement: Some collections required imagery improvements to meet customer satisfaction standards. This led to additional costs and delays in replenishing online jewelry images.

Lessons Learned:
1. Data-Driven Decision Making: Dive-X realized the power of analyzing data to make informed decisions about the inventory control processes. They learned the importance of tracking various metrics for strategic decision-making.

2. Continuous Improvement: By paying attention to customer feedback, the company acknowledged the need for constant jewelry image and description copy improvement and refinement of the dropship data management strategies.

3. Optimization Through Innovation: Analyzing website traffic and visitor behavior metrics helped Dive-X identify areas for improvement within their online store. They learned the importance of staying innovative to attract and retain customers.

Overall Impact:
Through the implementation of a comprehensive approach to data analysis and monitoring, Dive-X successfully optimized their dropship inventory management strategies. They achieved measurable outcomes in terms of increased sales, physical inventory reduction, cost reduction, and improved customer satisfaction. With the lessons learned, they were able to refine their approach further and continue to grow their customer base.

Now that we have reviewed the comprehensive approach implemented by Dive-X to optimize their dropship inventory management strategies, it is essential to highlight some key mistakes to avoid in order to ensure success in this process. These mistakes have been identified based on the experiences and challenges faced by Dive-X, and they provide valuable insights for any online retailer looking to enhance their inventory management strategies.

Typical Mistakes and How To Avoid Them

One common mistake that most people make in dropshipping is not closely tracking sales data. By monitoring overall sales volume and sales performance for individual jewelry designs, businesses can identify their best-selling items and understand customer demand patterns. The monitoring allows them to focus on promoting and expanding popular and profitable Jewelry designs and collections.

Another mistake is not monitoring jewelry design performance metrics, such as conversion rates, click-through rates, and average order value. Analyzing this data helps identify designs with high conversion rates, significant revenue, and images or entire collections that may need improvement or removal from inventory.

Ignoring customer feedback and reviews is another mistake. Monitoring customer satisfaction and identifying areas for improvement, such as adjusting Jewelry descriptions or enhancing quality, can help refine dropship inventory management strategies and ensure customer satisfaction.

Businesses should also pay attention to inventory interest and sales to identify slow-moving items and reduce premium image space losses. On the other hand, high turnover rates for specific designs can indicate strong demand and prompt design collection expansion.

Lastly, analyzing website traffic and visitor behavior metrics can provide insights into store performance. This data can help identify areas for improvement, such as optimizing jewelry placement or investing in targeted marketing campaigns.

In summary, businesses should establish a comprehensive approach to monitoring and analyzing dropship premium-space image metrics and data points to optimize their management strategies and increase sales.

Now that we have discussed the common mistakes to avoid in dropshipping, it is important to highlight the number one piece of advice that can help businesses avoid these pitfalls and succeed in their online dropship store management.

"Sales data: The ultimate gossip column in the world of dropshipping, telling you which products are the most popular."

My #1 Piece of Advice

Measure and analyze sales and online browsing data to identify popular items and remove underperforming ones. Utilize the power of The Dropship marketing and sales system to add and remove needed jewelry designs and collections that boost success in your struggling nautical and sea life jewelry online store.

Summary:

- Gain valuable insights into what is selling well and what is not to make informed decisions about expanding or contracting virtual inventory.
- Identify best-selling items and understand demand patterns to focus on promoting and stocking the most popular and profitable jewelry designs.
- Use jewelry performance metrics to identify high-converting and revenue-generating designs and improve or remove underperforming ones.
- Gauge customer satisfaction and make improvements based on feedback and reviews to ensure customer satisfaction.
- Track inventory interest to identify slow-moving items and optimize inventory presentation, while considering expanding inventory for high-demand jewelry.
- Analyze website traffic and visitor behavior metrics to optimize jewelry placement, user experience, and targeted marketing campaigns for increased conversions.

Quiz

1. By analyzing ____ data, businesses can identify their best-selling items and understand the demand patterns of their customer base.

2. Businesses should also monitor ____ metrics to gain insights into how well a specific product is performing.

3. Customer feedback is a valuable source of information that can help businesses ____ their dropship inventory management strategies.

4. Inventory turnover is a metric that calculates how quickly ____ is being sold and replenished.

5. Website traffic and visitor behavior metrics, such as the number of unique visitors, time spent on site, bounce rate, and conversion rate, can help businesses ____.

6. Businesses should establish a comprehensive approach to ____ and analyzing dropship inventory metrics.

7. By closely tracking sales data, product performance, customer feedback, inventory turnover, and website traffic metrics, businesses can ____.

8. Businesses can use customer feedback to ____ product quality or address any issues customers may have encountered.

9. High inventory turnover rates can indicate ____ demand, prompting businesses to consider expanding their inventory for those items.

10. By analyzing data points, businesses can ____ their sales and effectively grow their customer base.

Answer Key:
1. Sales
2. Product Performance
3. Refine
4. Inventory
5. Identify areas for improvement

6. Monitoring
7. Make data-driven decisions
8. Enhance
9. Strong
10. Increase

Now that we have discussed the essential metrics for dropshipping success, it's time to dive into the fascinating world of ocean sports and nautical retail jewelry, where we explore the latest trends and innovations that will keep businesses sailing smoothly toward growth and profitability - so grab your snorkel, and let's explore this exciting new chapter together!

CHAPTER 7. FLOW WITH THE DROPSHIPPING TIDES: STAYING AHEAD WITH TRENDS IN SEA LIFE AND OCEAN SPORTS RETAIL JEWELRY SALES

"With dropshipping, you can finally say goodbye to the risks of inventory management and hello to the smooth sailing with automated increased Sales!"

- "Discover the hottest trend in jewelry: sustainable and eco-friendly options that positively impact our oceans."
- "Get personal with your jewelry! Find out how you can customize and personalize your pieces to make them truly one-of-a-kind."
- "Less inventory is more Sales! Cut the Inventory to a minimum and show many more designs and collections by doing so."
- "Unlock the power of online shopping and expand your reach with a strong online presence and e-commerce capabilities."
- "Want to make a splash? Join forces with influential ocean sports, mermaids and nautical influencers to showcase your stunning jewelry collection."

In the ocean sports, sea life, and nautical retail jewelry industry, businesses should be aware of several key trends and innovations that can significantly impact their success. Understanding these trends and implementing them into their strategies can lead to increased sales and customer satisfaction. Here are some important trends to consider:

1. Sustainable and eco-friendly jewelry: With growing awareness of environmental issues, consumers are increasingly interested in

purchasing sustainably sourced and produced items. In the ocean sports and sea life industry, businesses should focus on offering jewelry made from recycled materials or responsibly sourced materials.

2. Customization and personalization: Consumers are now seeking unique and personalized products. Jewelry businesses should offer customization options where customers can personalize their items, such as adding initials, symbols, birthstones, or engraving meaningful messages. Customers feel a deeper connection with their jewelry. They're much more likely to purchase and share their story with their friends. The jewelry you sell is a marketing tool for your business as people constantly ask where they got that fantastic, customized piece of jewelry.

3. Sea Life designs: Sea life and nature-based jewelry designs have gained popularity in recent years. These important pieces are essential to spread an awareness of the beauty in and of the sea and can be worn on any occasion. Businesses should understand the power of their jewelry as an actual marketing tool. Consider your website engraved in your better-selling designs.

4. Online presence and e-commerce: The rise of online shopping has transformed the retail industry, including jewelry. To reach a wider audience and increase sales, businesses should establish dropshipping along with a solid online presence, including a user-friendly website and an active presence on social media platforms. Investing in e-commerce capabilities allows businesses to expand their customer base beyond their physical stores.

5. Influencer marketing: Influencer marketing has become a powerful tool for promoting products. Businesses should collaborate with popular influencers in the ocean sports and nautical field to showcase their jewelry and attract a more extensive customer base. Businesses can generate brand awareness and drive sales by partnering with influencers with a strong online presence and a relevant following.

By staying informed about these key trends and dropshipping innovations in the ocean sports, sea life, and nautical retail jewelry industry, businesses can better informed data-driven decisions about their jewelry collection offerings and marketing strategies. Adapting to these trends will help businesses stand out in the market, attract more customers, save money, and ultimately increase sales.

Now that you have learned about a few important trends and innovations in the ocean sports, sea life, and nautical retail jewelry industry, it's time to put that knowledge into action. I have created a checklist that will guide you in implementing these trends into your business strategies and staying ahead of the competition.

Checklist

Performance Evaluation Checklist:

1. Sustainable and Eco-friendly Jewelry:
- Has the business implemented sustainable and eco-friendly practices in sourcing and production?
- Have sales of sustainable and eco-friendly jewelry increased?
- Are customers actively seeking sustainable and eco-friendly jewelry options?

2. Customization and Personalization:
- Is the business offering customization options for customers?
- Are customers taking advantage of these customization options?
- Has the introduction of customization increased sales or customer satisfaction?

3. Dropshipping that expands Design Collections:
- Has the business expanded its range of jewelry collections?
- What are important relative designs that will sell well in your area?
- Can the business properly keep up with demand for expanded

collections?

4. Online Presence and E-commerce:
- Has the business established a solid online presence, including a user-friendly website and active social media presence?
- Have online sales increased since implementing an e-commerce platform?
- Are customers engaging with the business's online platforms?
- Are you currently using a Dropshipping model?

5. Influencer Marketing:
- Has the business collaborated with influencers in the ocean sports, sea life and nautical niche markets?
- Has this collaboration resulted in increased brand awareness and sales?
- How effective has influencer marketing been in attracting a more extensive customer base?

Additionally, the evaluation checklist should also include performance metrics such as sales revenue, customer satisfaction ratings, website traffic, social media engagement, and customer feedback to track the success and impact of implementing these trends and innovations.

Now that we have reviewed the performance evaluation checklist, let's take a look at some examples that demonstrate how these trends and innovations have been implemented and their impact on the business.

Examples

Sustainable packaging: In addition to sustainable materials used in jewelry, businesses should also consider eco-friendly packaging options. This may include using recycled or biodegradable materials for jewelry boxes and bags, reducing plastic packaging, or using innovative packaging designs that minimize waste.

Storytelling and brand narratives: Consumers are always

interested in a story or valuable symbolic meaning behind the designs they purchase. Jewelry businesses should focus on creating compelling brand narratives and sharing the stories of their designs and collections. These stories could include highlighting the craftsmanship behind each piece, showcasing the inspiration from the ocean or sea life, or emphasizing a symbol or cultural value, and enhancing a deeper connection along with the value and energy of the precious metals. They all add up to a meaningful sale.

Collaborations and sponsorships with conservation organizations: In the ocean sports and sea life industry, businesses can form partnerships or alliances with conservation organizations to highlight their commitment to protecting marine ecosystems. This not only raises awareness about important conservation efforts but also provides customers with a sense of contributing to a greater cause when purchasing jewelry.

Social responsibility and ethical practices: Consumers are becoming more conscious of businesses' social and ethical practices. Jewelry businesses should be transparent about their manufacturing processes, ensuring fair labor practices and avoiding environmentally harmful materials. Incorporating social responsibility into their business practices can attract socially conscious consumers and enhance the company's reputation.

Innovative materials and designs: Jewelry businesses should stay updated on new materials and design trends in the industry. For example, embracing sustainable alternatives to traditional diamonds and gemstones, such as lab-grown diamonds or recycled silver, can appeal to environmentally conscious consumers. Additionally, experimenting with unique and unconventional jewelry designs can help businesses stand out and cater to customers seeking something different and eye-catching.

Social media storytelling: Utilizing social media platforms like Instagram or TikTok to tell engaging stories about the brand and its products can help jewelry businesses reach a wider audience and build a loyal customer base. Creating visually appealing content, collaborating with influencers, and running engaging campaigns can generate buzz and create a strong online presence.

Now that we have explored various strategies for sustainable and ethical practices in the jewelry industry, let's dive into a case study that showcases how a jewelry business successfully implemented these principles to differentiate themselves in the market.

Case Study

Case Study: The Impact of Measuring Trends in Online Jewelry Sales

Background:
SEA Jewelry is an online retail store specializing in ocean sports, sea life, and nautical-inspired jewelry. They have identified the importance of measuring trends in the marketplace and jewelry designs to optimize their product offerings and attract more customers. By combining data on what is selling in the marketplace with customer preferences, SEA Jewelry aims to enhance its sales and overall success.

Actions Taken:
1. Data Collection: SEA Jewelry implemented a robust data collection system to track sales, website analytics, and customer preferences. They collected data on the jewelry items that were selling well and the ones that were not generating much interest.

2. Identifying Trends: By analyzing the data collected, SEA Jewelry identified key trends in the industry. They discovered that sustainable and eco-friendly jewelry, customization and personalization, meaningful symbolic designs, and an online presence were popular among their target customers.

3. Product Development: Based on the identified trends, SEA Jewelry introduced a new line of sustainable and eco-friendly jewelry, including pieces made from recycled silver, responsibly sourced pearls, and created gemstones. They also introduced customization options, allowing customers to add initials, birthstones, or engraved messages on their jewelry items. Additionally, SEA Jewelry expanded their collection with a range of culturally connected designs.

4. Online Presence Enhancement: ABC Jewelry invested in improving their online presence by revamping their website and optimizing it for user-friendliness. They also increased their social media presence with regular updates and engaging content to attract a wider audience.

5. Influencer Collaboration: To further promote their jewelry, SEA Jewelry collaborated with popular influencers and several mermaids in the ocean sports and nautical fields. These influencers showcased SEA Jewelry's exclusive designs on their social media platforms, generating brand awareness and driving sales.

Outcomes:
1. Increased Sales: SEA Jewelry experienced a significant increase in sales following the implementation of their data-driven strategies supported by a dropshipping inventory reduction system on the backend. The introduction of sustainable and eco-friendly jewelry, customization options, and meaningful designs resonated with their target customers, leading to higher sales volumes.

2. Improved Customer Satisfaction: The customization options and minimalist designs allowed customers to feel a deeper connection with their jewelry, resulting in improved customer satisfaction and loyalty.

3. Expanded Customer Base: With an enhanced online presence

and influencer collaborations, SEA Jewelry was able to attract a more extensive customer base beyond their physical store. They used dropshipping to deliver to a worldwide market, further improving the online shopping experience and increasing customer confidence in purchasing from anywhere in the world.

Challenges Faced:
1. Adaptation and Innovation: Implementing new trends and innovations required ABC Jewelry to adapt quickly and continuously innovate their product offerings and marketing strategies. Their experienced dropshipping partner, also knowledgeable in their need and desires, played a significant role in fully supporting their efforts, making these moves attainable and achievable much faster than they had expected.

2. Market Saturation: The ocean sports, sea life, and nautical retail jewelry industry is highly competitive, with many players offering similar products. SEA Jewelry had to differentiate itself by staying ahead of the trends and continuously analyzing customer preferences. Their sterling silver and gold jewelry lines also have way above-average unique designs, beauty, finish detail, and overall quality. They stood out. They showed up differently than the masses, helping their brand every step of the way.

Lessons Learned:
1. Market Awareness: Keeping track of trends and innovations is crucial to staying competitive in the retail industry, but even more important is getting ahead of the wave and leading while others try to catch up. Regular data analysis helps in making informed decisions about jewelry design, research and marketing strategies.

2. Customer-Centric Approach: Offering customization options and meaningful designs provided customers with personalized and versatile jewelry options, resulting in increased customer satisfaction and sales.

Overall Assessment:
The implementation of data-driven strategies and an

understanding of industry trends have had a significant impact on SEA Jewelry's success. By measuring what was selling in the marketplace, identifying trends, and combining these numbers with customer preferences while adding their own inner creativity to the mix, ABC Jewelry has been able to add popular items and remove those that were not performing well swiftly with minimal effort with the help of the dropshipping system they implemented. This approach has helped them optimize their jewelry design offerings to attract a wider band of interested customers while consistently increasing sales and service. The company's focus on sustainability, personalization, and a strong online presence has ensured they remain competitive in the ocean sports, sea life, and nautical retail jewelry.

Now that we have reviewed the case study and seen the positive outcomes of ABC Jewelry's data-driven strategies, let's take a closer look at some common mistakes to avoid to maximize these strategies' effectiveness. By being aware of these pitfalls, we can ensure a smooth implementation and further enhance the success of our online jewelry business.

Typical Mistakes And How To Avoid Them

Based on the material provided, some mistakes that most people make in the ocean sports, sea life, and nautical retail jewelry industry include:

1. Ignoring sustainability: Many businesses fail to recognize the growing awareness of environmental issues and the importance of sustainable and eco-friendly practices. To avoid this mistake, businesses should focus on offering jewelry made from recycled materials or responsibly sourced materials.

2. Neglecting customization: Businesses often overlook the demand for personalized products. To avoid this mistake, jewelry businesses should offer customization options such as adding initials, birthstones, or engraving meaningful messages, allowing

customers to feel a deeper connection with their jewelry.

3. Overlooking meaningful design: The popularity of expressive and symbolic jewelry designs is often underestimated. To avoid this mistake, businesses should consider offering a variety of jewelry collection options to cater to the growing demand for deeply meaningful, culturally connected and symbolic designs.

4. Neglecting the online presence: Some businesses fail to recognize the impact of online shopping on the retail industry. To avoid this mistake, businesses should establish a strong online presence, including a user-friendly website and an active presence on social media platforms. Implementing a simple-to-use Dropshipping system for inventory management savings and efficiency, coupled with a worldwide delivery reach, is necessary today to ensure a business that accelerates and continually builds its brand momentum. Investing in e-commerce capabilities is also crucial for expanding the customer base beyond physical stores.

5. Ignoring influencer marketing: The power of influencer marketing is often overlooked by businesses in this industry. To avoid this mistake, businesses should collaborate with popular influencers in the ocean sports and nautical field to showcase their jewelry and attract a larger customer base.

By avoiding these common mistakes and adopting the trends and innovations discussed, businesses can exponentially increase their success in the ocean sports, sea life, and nautical retail jewelry industry.

Now that we have discussed the mistakes to avoid in the ocean sports, sea life, and nautical retail jewelry industry, it is essential to consider the #1 piece of advice that can help businesses thrive in this industry.

My #1 Piece of Advice

My #1 advice for struggling dive, surf, ocean sports, and beach resort sea life jewelry gift shops with an online store is to understand the power of measuring what is selling in the marketplace and the jewelry designs being looked at and sold in your online store. Combine these numbers and identify trends to add more popular items and remove the items visitors are not looking at, avoiding wasting valuable space and time. This is a key element of success in the Jewelry Dropship marketing and sales system.

Summary:

- Embrace sustainability: Offer jewelry made from recycled materials or responsibly sourced materials, like pearls from sustainable farms, to meet the growing demand for eco-friendly products.
- Personalize your pieces: Allow customers to add initials, birthstones, or engrave meaningful messages on their jewelry for a unique and personal touch that strengthens their connection to the product.
- Keep it meaningful: Cater to the rising popularity of expressive designs by offering symbolic, creative pieces that can be worn for any occasion.
- Go online and go big: Establish a solid online presence with a user-friendly website, Worldwide dropshipping and active social media platforms to reach a wider audience. At the same time, you expand your customer base beyond physical stores and get a grip on inventory control responsibilities and reduction.
- Collaborate with influencers: Partner with popular influencers in the ocean sports, mermaids and nautical field to showcase your jewelry, generating brand awareness and driving sales.

Quiz

1. Sustainable and eco-friendly jewelry is an important trend in

the ocean sports, sea life, and nautical retail jewelry industry. True or False?

2. Customization and personalization allow customers to feel a deeper connection with their jewelry. True or False?

3. Investing in e-commerce capabilities is unnecessary for businesses to reach a wider audience. True or False?

4. Influencer marketing is an effective tool for promoting jewelry designs in ocean sports, sea life awareness and the nautical world. True or False?

5. Dropshipping is a crucial system implementing data tracking technology for inventory reduction and significant cost savings for those who shop online. True or False?

6. Adapting to key trends and innovations in the ocean sports, sea life, and nautical retail jewelry industry will help businesses stand out in the market. True or False?

7. Meaningful symbolic designs have become popular in recent years. True or False?

8. Businesses should not establish a strong online presence to reach a wider audience. True or False?

9. Customers are not interested in purchasing items that are sustainably sourced and produced. True or False?

10. Pearls are not sourced from sustainable pearl farms. True or False?

Answer Key:
1. True
2. True
3. False
4. True
5. True
6. True

7. True
8. False
9. False
10. False

"Now that we have explored the key trends and innovations in the ocean sports, sea life, and nautical retail jewelry industry, it is vital for businesses to understand how they can utilize customer feedback and preferences to curate collections that meet the tastes and preferences of their target market. Keep reading to discover the invaluable insights and strategies that will help your business thrive in today's competitive market."

CHAPTER 8. FROM OCEAN TO E-COMMERCE: CONQUER THE MARKET WITH THE ADDITION OF EXPANDED DROPSHIP ONLINE

"Ocean Jewels went from a sinking ship to a thriving treasure chest with dropshipping!"

- "Discover how Ocean Jewels, a resort jewelry gift shop, skyrocketed their success by incorporating dropshipping into their business model."
- "From limited stock availability to high inventory costs, learn how dropshipping helped Ocean Jewels overcome numerous business obstacles."
- "Find out how dropshipping enabled Ocean Jewels to greatly expand their product range, offering a wide selection of jewelry gifts for diverse customer preferences."
- "Learn how dropshipping reduced overhead costs for Ocean Jewels, allowing them to allocate more funds towards marketing efforts and driving increased sales."
- "Explore how dropshipping improved order fulfillment for Ocean Jewels, leading to faster shipping and enhanced customer satisfaction."

Numerous businesses have achieved great success by implementing a dropshipping service for their retail jewelry gifts. One notable success story is that of Ocean Jewels, a resort jewelry gift shop that experienced tremendous growth after incorporating dropshipping into their business model.

Before implementing dropshipping, Ocean Jewels faced several challenges, including limited stock availability, high inventory costs, and the inability to offer a wide selection of products; by leveraging the dropshipping model, they were able to overcome these obstacles and achieve significant results.

First and foremost, dropshipping allowed Ocean Jewels to expand its product range significantly. By partnering with multiple reputable suppliers, they gained access to a much more comprehensive selection of jewelry gifts, including mid-level to high-end options. This partnership enabled them to cater to a broader range of customers with diverse tastes and preferences, making their store more attractive to potential buyers.

Moreover, by eliminating the need to hold inventory, Ocean Jewels significantly reduced its overhead costs. They no longer needed to invest in large quantities of stock upfront, which helped improve their cash flow and overall financial stability. This cost-saving benefit allowed them to allocate more funds towards marketing efforts, driving more traffic to their online store and increasing their sales.

Additionally, dropshipping allowed Ocean Jewels to fulfill customer orders more efficiently and promptly. Instead of relying on their own storage and shipping infrastructure, they leveraged their suppliers' logistics capabilities. This allowed for faster order processing and shipping, leading to improved customer satisfaction and increased customer loyalty.

Furthermore, by implementing a dropshipping service, Ocean Jewels enhanced their online presence and visibility. They were able to collaborate with their suppliers to create high-quality product images and descriptions, ensuring that their online store showcased the beauty and uniqueness of each jewelry gift. Coupled with well-executed digital marketing strategies, this led to increased brand awareness, higher website traffic, and, ultimately, more sales.

In conclusion, the success story of Ocean Jewels demonstrates the immense benefits that businesses can derive from implementing a dropshipping service for their retail jewelry gifts. By expanding their product range, reducing overhead costs, improving order fulfillment, and enhancing their online presence, they could attract more customers, increase sales, and establish themselves as a dominant player in the market. If other struggling dive, surf, ocean sports, beach resorts, and sea life jewelry gift shops want to achieve similar success, adopting dropshipping could be a game-changing strategy.

Now that we have explored the success story of Ocean Jewels and the benefits they obtained from implementing dropshipping, it's time to dive deeper into how other dive resorts and sea life jewelry shops can achieve similar results. To help you get started, I have created a comprehensive checklist that outlines the key steps and considerations for incorporating dropshipping into your business model.

Checklist

Preparations Checklist for Implementing Dropshipping for Retail Jewelry Gifts:

1. Research and identify a proven, reputable supplier in the jewelry industry that offers exceptional dropshipping services. Look for a dropship supplier that has a wide range of designs and offers good-quality jewelry gifts.

2. Analyze your current inventory and identify the Collections that are in high demand and those that are not selling well. Determine the gaps in your product range that can be filled through dropshipping.

3. Evaluate your current financial situation and calculate the potential cost savings from eliminating the need to hold more inventory than necessary. Determine how these savings can be allocated towards marketing efforts to increase sales.

4. Develop a marketing strategy that focuses on driving more

traffic to your online store. Consider utilizing digital marketing techniques such as search engine optimization (SEO), social media marketing, and email marketing to enhance your online presence and increase brand awareness.

5. Collaborate with your chosen supplier to create high-quality jewelry images and descriptions that showcase the beauty and uniqueness of each jewelry gift. This will help attract customers and persuade them to make a purchase.

6. Ensure your website is optimized for easy navigation and a user-friendly experience. Make sure it is mobile responsive and has a secure payment gateway to instill customer trust and confidence.

7. Implement a reliable order fulfillment process by leveraging your suppliers' logistics capabilities. Establish clear agreements with your dropship supplier regarding order processing and shipping times to ensure prompt delivery and customer satisfaction.

8. Train your customer service team to efficiently handle customer inquiries and complaints. Provide them with the necessary information about your dropshipping suppliers and their products so that they can assist customers effectively.

9. Monitor and evaluate the performance of your dropshipping service regularly. Keep track of sales, customer feedback, and any issues that may arise. Make adjustments and improvements to your dropshipping strategy as needed.

10. Continuously update your jewelry collections by exploring new designs and unique niche markets, plus adding trending jewelry gifts in Gold. Stay updated with industry trends and customer preferences to ensure your jewelry offerings remain relevant and appealing.

By following this checklist, businesses can properly prepare for implementing dropshipping for their retail jewelry gifts, similar to the success story of Ocean Jewels.

Now that we have gone through the checklist for implementing dropshipping for retail jewelry gifts, let's take a look at some examples that align with each of the checklist items.

Examples

Here are a few additional examples to help illustrate the benefits of dropshipping for retail jewelry giftshops:

1. Sparkling Seas Boutique:
Sparkling Seas Boutique is a small, local jewelry gift shop that struggled with limited resources and inventory. By implementing a dropshipping service, they could dramatically expand their collections and offer a wider selection of jewelry options, including customizable pieces. This service attracted a more extensive customer base and increased their sales, ultimately allowing them to open a second location. When they added the gold jewelry to their store, that's when their business really took off!

2. Elegant Treasures:
Elegant Treasures, an established jewelry gift shop, faced the challenge of managing inventory costs and management systems. By partnering with a proven, reputable dropshipping supplier, they were able to eliminate these issues and reduce their overhead costs significantly. This freed up resources they could reinvest in marketing efforts, increasing brand exposure and considerably boosting their online sales.

3. Gemstone Gallery:
Gemstone Gallery, an online jewelry retailer, struggled with slow order processing and shipping times due to their lack of a dedicated logistics infrastructure. By integrating a dropshipping service into their business model, they could leverage their suppliers' efficient fulfillment processes, leading to faster delivery and improved customer satisfaction. This resulted in higher

customer retention rates and positive reviews, further enhancing their reputation and driving more sales.

4. Nature's Charms:

Nature's Charms, a nature-themed jewelry gift shop, wanted to expand their product offerings to include eco-friendly and sustainable jewelry options. By partnering with an eco-conscious dropshipping supplier, they were able to source and offer a wide range of environmentally friendly jewelry pieces. This not only aligned with their brand values but also attracted a niche customer base that valued sustainability, resulting in increased sales and brand loyalty.

5. Jewel Fusions:

Jewel Fusions, a jewelry gift shop specializing in unique, handcrafted pieces, struggled with marketing and reaching a wider audience beyond their local market. By collaborating with a solid dropshipping supplier with established online platforms and a strong customer base, they could expand their reach and sell their products to customers worldwide. This global exposure led to a significant increase in sales and helped establish Jewel Fusions as a reputable brand in the industry.

Now that we have explored several examples of how dropshipping has benefited retail jewelry gift shops, let's dive into a case study that further illustrates the advantages of implementing a dropshipping service.

Case Study

Case Study: Ocean Jewels - Transforming a Beach Resort Jewelry Giftshop through Dropshipping

Overview: Ocean Jewels is a resort jewelry gift shop that experienced exceptional growth by incorporating dropshipping into their business model. Prior to implementing dropshipping, the company faced challenges with limited stock availability, high inventory costs, and a restricted product range.

Challenges Faced:

1. Limited stock availability: Ocean Jewels struggled to maintain a diverse inventory due to upfront investment in stock.

2. High inventory costs: Holding a large quantity of stock required significant financial investment, impacting their cash flow.

3. Restricted jewelry collection: The limited product range made it challenging to cater to a diverse customer base and meet their preferences and tastes.

Actions Taken:

1. Partnered with a reputable supplier: By collaborating with an experienced, reputable supplier with 20+ years of dropshipping experience, Ocean Jewels gained access to a broader selection of jewelry gifts, including mid-level to high-end options, including gold, which they could have never afforded to stock.

2. Implemented dropshipping model: By leveraging the dropshipping model, Ocean Jewels eliminated the need for inventory and time to manage stock, reducing overhead costs and improving cash flow.

3. Enhanced online presence: Collaborating with their supplier, Ocean Jewels created high-quality jewelry images and descriptions in addition to the Images and descriptions the supplier offered them at no charge, improving their online store's visibility, value, and attractiveness. Many new repeat clients came on board.

4. Allocated more funds to marketing: The cost-saving benefits of dropshipping allowed Ocean Jewels to invest more in marketing efforts, driving increased website traffic and sales.

Measurable Outcomes:

1. Expanded Jewelry collections: Ocean Jewels was able to offer a broader selection of jewelry gifts to cater to diverse customer preferences, attracting a wider customer base and a higher-end clientele.

2. Reduced overhead costs: By eliminating the need for inventory, tracking and restocking, the company experienced significant

cost savings, improving their financial stability.

3. Improved order fulfillment: Leveraging suppliers' logistics capabilities enabled Ocean Jewels to process and ship customer orders more efficiently, enhancing customer satisfaction and loyalty.

4. Increased online visibility and sales: The enhanced online presence, coupled with effective digital marketing strategies, resulted in higher website traffic, brand awareness, and, ultimately, increased sales.

Challenges Faced:

1. Supplier reliability: Ocean Jewels faced occasional challenges with suppliers, including delayed shipments or product quality issues, impacting customer satisfaction and the company's reputation, until they found one with a proven and long track record of reliability.

2. Striking a balance with inventory: With almost no inventory on hand, the company had collections and timely order fulfillment.

Lessons Learned:

1. Establish strong supplier partnerships: Building relationships with a reliable supplier is crucial to ensure consistent product quality and timely order fulfillment.

2. Regularly review and analyze supplier performance: Regular assessments of supplier reliability and quality are vital to maintaining customer satisfaction and the company's reputation.

3. Continuous marketing efforts are essential: While dropshipping provides many benefits, a proactive marketing strategy is necessary to drive traffic and increase sales.

Overall Impact:

Ocean Jewels achieved significant growth and established themselves as a dominant player in the marketplace by incorporating dropshipping. Through an expanded jewelry range, reduced overhead costs, improved order fulfillment, and an enhanced online presence, they attracted more customers, increased sales, and improved their financial stability. The success of Ocean Jewels serves as a compelling case study for struggling dive, surf, ocean sports, and resort sea life jewelry gift shops, considering dropshipping as an absolute game-changing strategy.

Now that we have examined the success of Ocean Jewels in transforming their resort jewelry gift shop through dropshipping, let's take a look at some of the critical mistakes to avoid in implementing this strategy. By learning from these mistakes, struggling dive, surf, ocean sports, beach resort and sea life jewelry gift shops can effectively harness the benefits of dropshipping and avoid potential pitfalls.

Typical Mistakes And How To Avoid Them

Based on the material covered here, some common mistakes that people make in the area of dropshipping for retail jewelry gifts include:

1. Not partnering with a proven, reputable supplier: By building a close relationship for success allows for the supplier to give personal service and help their jewelry ranges expand and be the very best possible. They may not only cater to the diverse preferences of customers but now start to attract a new higher-end customer base. There is enormous value in building a solid relationship with a business dropship supplier that has a track record and resources.

2. Failing to reduce overhead costs: Holding inventory can be costly for businesses, especially if they have had it for some time or have to invest in large quantities of stock upfront. To avoid this mistake, businesses should consider dropshipping, eliminating the need to hold inventory and helping improve cash flow.

3. Neglecting order fulfillment efficiency: Businesses that rely on their own storage and shipping infrastructure may experience delays in order processing and shipping. To avoid this, leveraging the logistics capabilities of suppliers through dropshipping allows for a wider choice of collections. It leads to faster and more

efficient order fulfillment, improving customer satisfaction and loyalty.

4. Overlooking the importance of online presence: In today's digital age, having a strong online presence is crucial for businesses. Neglecting to enhance their online store with high-quality product images and descriptions and effective digital marketing strategies can limit brand awareness and website traffic. To avoid this mistake, businesses should collaborate with suppliers to showcase the beauty and uniqueness of each jewelry gift and invest in digital marketing efforts.

By avoiding these common mistakes and implementing dropshipping for retail jewelry gifts, businesses can expand their jewelry ranges, reduce costs, improve order fulfillment, and enhance their online presence to attract more customers, increase sales, and establish themselves in the market.

With these mistakes to avoid in mind, it is crucial to implement the #1 piece of advice: prioritize building solid partnerships with multiple reputable suppliers.

My #1 Piece of Advice

The key advice for struggling dive, surf, ocean sports, beach resort and sea life jewelry gift shop owners and online store managers in the mid-level to high-end market is to focus on unique and beautifully crafted jewelry lines in both sterling silver and gold that genuinely capture the essence of the ocean and sea life. It will grow your sales and business to the heights you've always dreamed of.

Summary:

- Expand your jewelry collections: By implementing dropshipping, you can offer a more comprehensive selection of jewelry designs and collections, catering to a broader range of customers with diverse tastes and preferences. Include both fine sterling silver and gold jewelry collections to reach all buyers' wants and desires.

- Reduce overhead costs: With dropshipping, you eliminate the need for significant upfront investments in inventory, freeing up funds for marketing efforts and improving overall financial stability.
- Improve order fulfillment: Leveraging your suppliers' logistics capabilities enables faster processing and shipping, increasing customer satisfaction and loyalty.
- Enhance online presence: Collaborate with suppliers to create high-quality jewelry images and descriptions, coupled with well-executed digital marketing strategies, to increase brand awareness, website traffic, and, ultimately, sales.
- Achieve success like Ocean Jewels: Follow in the footsteps of a successful jewelry gift shop by adopting dropshipping and positioning yourself as a dominant player in the market.

Quiz

Quiz Questions:

1. What business experienced tremendous growth after incorporating dropshipping into their business model?

2. What challenges did Ocean Jewels face before implementing dropshipping?

3. How did dropshipping allow Ocean Jewels to expand their product range?

4. What was one of the cost-saving benefits that Ocean Jewels gained from leveraging dropshipping?

5. How did dropshipping enable Ocean Jewels to fulfill customer orders more efficiently and promptly?

6. What did Ocean Jewels do to enhance their online presence and

visibility?

7. How did Ocean Jewels attract more customers and increase sales?

8. What is the main benefit of adopting a dropshipping service for retail jewelry gift shops?

9. What type of businesses can benefit from implementing a dropshipping service?

10. What type of ocean-themed jewelry gift shop is used as an example in this material?

Answer Key:
1 - Ocean Jewels
2 - Limited stock availability, high inventory costs, and the inability to offer a wide selection of jewelry collections,
3 - By partnering with multiple reputable suppliers
4 - Improving their cash flow and overall financial stability
5 - By leveraging their suppliers' logistics capabilities
6 - Collaborated with their suppliers to create high-quality product images and descriptions
7 - By implementing well-executed digital marketing strategies
8 - To achieve significant results and establish themselves as a dominant player in the market
9- Retail jewelry giftshops
10 - Beach resort jewelry giftshop

Now that we have seen the potential of Dropshipping in the retail jewelry gifts business, let's dive into how companies in the ocean sports, sea life, and nautical retail jewelry and gift sales can amplify their success by incorporating stunning Sterling Silver and Exquisite Gold jewelry into their cyber inventory. Get ready to uncover a world of possibilities and discover how these precious metals can make waves in your business!

CHAPTER 9. MASTERING SUCCESS: ESSENTIAL STEPS FOR IMPLEMENTING EFFECTIVE DROPSHIPPING STRATEGIES

"Efficiency is the heartbeat of dropshipping, and establishing a seamless order fulfillment process is essential in ensuring customer satisfaction and repeat business."

- Discover the secrets behind dropshipping fine sterling silver and gold jewelry for your dive, surf, or sea life beach resort store.
- Unleash your creativity with an outstanding selection of beautifully crafted and exclusive designs that will set your store apart.
- Elevate your online store with stunning product listings that showcase each piece's intricate details and quality craftsmanship.
- Unlock the power of competitive pricing strategies while maintaining profitability and covering expenses.
- Dive into success with streamlined order fulfillment and a comprehensive marketing strategy that will attract customers who value style and quality.

To effectively implement the sterling silver and gold jewelry dropshipping strategies outlined in my book, owners, operators, and managers of dive, surf, ocean sports, beach resort, and sea life jewelry shops with online stores should follow a series of high-level steps and actions. These steps are designed to maximize the benefits of dropshipping and optimize sales, profitability, and customer base expansion.

1. Research and select a reliable supplier: The first step is to thoroughly research and identify a reputable supplier who

specializes in dropshipping fine sterling silver and gold jewelry with an extensive inventory of choices available to you. This research is crucial to ensure the quality, authenticity, variety in collections and timely delivery of the jewelry. Look for suppliers with a strong track record, positive customer reviews, and reasonable pricing.

2. Develop a comprehensive product selection: With dropshipping, the advantage lies in offering a wide variety of jewelry products without the need for physical inventory. It is essential to curate a unique and extensive collection of beautifully crafted sterling silver and gold jewelry to cater to the preferences and tastes of a diverse customer base. Focus on offering high-quality and exclusive designs that differentiate your store from competitors.

3. Optimize jewelry collection listings: Pay attention to the presentation and appeal of your jewelry listings. Use high-resolution images that highlight the intricate details and craftsmanship of each piece. Write accurate and compelling jewelry descriptions that emphasize the quality and uniqueness of the jewelry. Include relevant details such as metal type, gemstones, dimensions, and any special features.

4. Implement effective pricing strategies: Consider a pricing structure that allows for competitive pricing while maintaining profitability. Analyze market trends, competitor pricing, and customer preferences to determine optimal price points. Additionally, factor in the costs associated with dropshipping, such as supplier fees and shipping charges, to ensure you set prices that cover expenses and generate a suitable profit margin.

5. Streamline the order fulfillment process: Establish a seamless process to handle orders once they are placed. Communicate effectively with suppliers, ensuring they have sufficient stock and can ship items promptly. Integrate inventory management systems to track product availability and provide real-time

updates to your customers. Promptly address any order issues or delays that may arise to maintain a positive customer experience.

6. Market and promote your store: Implement a comprehensive marketing strategy to drive traffic to your online store. Leverage various channels such as social media, email marketing, content marketing, organic and paid advertising to reach your target audience. Emphasize the unique designs and high quality of your sterling silver and gold jewelry to attract customers who value craftsmanship and style.

7. Analyze data and refine strategies: Continuously monitor and analyze sales data, customer feedback, and market trends to refine your dropshipping system. Identify your best-selling items, customer preferences, and opportunities for expansion. Based on these insights, adjust your product selection, marketing efforts, and pricing strategies to continually improve sales and profitability.

In conclusion, successfully implementing sterling silver and gold jewelry dropshipping strategies requires thorough research, careful supplier selection, a comprehensive product selection, effective pricing strategies, streamlined order fulfillment, strategic marketing, and constant analysis and refinement. By following these high-level steps and actions, owners, operators, and managers can maximize the benefits of dropshipping, increase sales, reduce inventory costs, and expand their customer base.

"In the world of dropshipping, success lies in the hands of those who curate unique and exquisite collections that speak to the desires of their diverse customer base."

Now that you have read the article on effectively implementing sterling silver and gold jewelry dropshipping strategies, it's time to put that knowledge into action. To help you get started, I have created a checklist that outlines the key steps and actions you need to take in order to maximize the benefits of dropshipping and optimize your sales and profitability.

Checklist

Onboarding Checklist for Dropshipping Jewelry Businesses:

1. Research and select a reliable supplier:
- Conduct thorough research to identify reputable suppliers specializing in dropshipping fine sterling silver and gold jewelry with a large selection of niche jewelry collections available in both precious metals.
- Look for suppliers with a strong track record, positive customer reviews, and reasonable pricing.

2. Develop a comprehensive product selection:
- Curate a unique and extensive collection of beautifully crafted sterling silver and gold jewelry to cater to a diverse customer base.
- Focus on offering high-quality, exclusive designs that differentiate your store from competitors.

3. Optimize product listings:
- Use high-resolution images highlighting each piece's intricate details and craftsmanship.
- Write accurate and compelling product descriptions that emphasize the quality and uniqueness of the jewelry.
- Include relevant details such as metal type, gemstones, dimensions, and any special features.
- Ask your dropship manufacturer for images and jewelry descriptions they have available to you.

4. Implement effective pricing strategies:
- Analyze market trends, competitor pricing, and customer preferences to determine optimal price points.
- Consider the costs associated with dropshipping, such as supplier fees and shipping charges, when setting prices.

5. Streamline the order fulfillment process:
- Establish a seamless process to handle orders once they are

placed, communicating effectively with suppliers.

- Integrate inventory management systems to track product availability and provide real-time updates to customers.
- Address any order issues or delays promptly to maintain a positive customer experience.

6. Market and promote your store:
- Implement a comprehensive marketing strategy to drive traffic to your online store.
- Leverage various channels such as social media, email marketing, content marketing, and paid advertising.
- Emphasize the unique designs and the high quality of your jewelry to attract customers who value craftsmanship and style.

7. Analyze data and refine strategies:
- Continuously monitor and analyze sales data, customer feedback, and market trends.
- Identify best-selling items, customer preferences, and opportunities for expansion.
- Adjust your jewelry selection, marketing efforts, and pricing strategies based on insights gained through data collected to continually improve sales and profitability.

By following these steps, owners, operators, and managers can maximize the benefits of dropshipping jewelry, optimize sales, profitability, and expand their customer base.

"The key to effective dropshipping is not just finding reliable suppliers, but finding partners who align with your values and deliver the quality and authenticity your customers expect."

Now that we have gone through the onboarding checklist for dropshipping jewelry businesses, let's take a look at some examples that demonstrate how each of these steps can be implemented effectively.

Examples

Example 1:

Sarah owns a beach resort gift shop located in a popular surfing destination. She decides to implement the dropshipping strategies outlined in the book to expand her online store's inventory. After conducting thorough research, Sarah selects a reputable supplier that specializes in sterling silver and gold jewelry. She ensures they have a strong track record, positive customer reviews, and reasonable pricing. Sarah then curates a collection of beautifully crafted jewelry, including unique designs that cater to the diverse preferences of her customers. She optimizes her product listings by using high-resolution images and writing accurate and compelling descriptions that emphasize the quality and exclusivity of the jewelry. Sarah carefully considers market trends, competitor pricing, and customer preferences to establish a competitive pricing structure that maintains profitability. She sets up a seamless order fulfillment process, communicates effectively with her supplier, and integrates an inventory management system to provide real-time updates to her customers. To promote her store, Sarah implements a comprehensive marketing strategy that includes social media campaigns, email marketing, content marketing, and paid advertising. She emphasizes the unique designs and high quality of her sterling silver and gold jewelry to attract customers who value craftsmanship and style. Sarah continuously monitors sales data, customer feedback, and market trends to refine her dropshipping strategies. She identifies her best-selling items, customer preferences, and opportunities for expansion. Sarah adjusts her jewelry selection, marketing efforts, and pricing strategies based on these insights to improve sales and profitability.

Example 2:

David manages a dive shop in a popular seaside town. He wants to expand his business by offering a more comprehensive range of jewelry options to his customers. David decides to implement the dropshipping strategies outlined in the book and begins by researching reliable suppliers. He finds a supplier with a strong reputation for fine sterling silver and gold jewelry and positive customer reviews. David curates a comprehensive product selection that includes beautifully crafted pieces suitable for divers and ocean sports enthusiasts. He optimizes his product listings by using high-resolution images that showcase the intricate details and craftsmanship of each piece. David also writes accurate and compelling product descriptions, highlighting the quality and uniqueness of the jewelry. Taking into account market trends and competitor pricing, David implements an effective pricing strategy that allows for competitive pricing while maintaining profitability. He factors in dropshipping costs, such as supplier fees and shipping charges, to set prices that cover expenses and generate a suitable profit margin. David sets up a streamlined order fulfillment process, ensuring clear communication with his supplier and integrating inventory management systems to track product availability. He promptly addresses any order issues or delays to provide a positive customer experience. To market his store, David implements a comprehensive marketing strategy that includes social media campaigns, content marketing, and paid advertising targeted towards divers and ocean sports enthusiasts. He emphasizes the high quality and exclusive designs of his sterling silver and gold jewelry to attract customers with a taste for unique pieces. David constantly analyzes sales data, customer feedback, and market trends to refine his dropshipping strategies. He identifies his best-selling items, customer preferences, and opportunities for expansion, making adjustments to his jewelry selection and marketing efforts to continually improve sales and profitability.

Based on these examples, Sarah and David have successfully implemented dropshipping strategies to expand their businesses and enhance their jewelry collection offerings. They have both utilized effective marketing strategies to attract their target customers and have continuously monitored market trends and customer preferences to improve sales and profitability. Now, let's take a look at the case study I have created to further explore the benefits and challenges of dropshipping in a specific scenario.

Case Study

Case Study: Maximizing the Benefits of Dropshipping Fine Sterling Silver & Gold Jewelry

Background:
Maximizing the benefits of dropshipping has been a key focus for the owners, operators, and managers of a luxury jewelry store specializing in sterling silver and gold pieces. The store, located in a popular beach resort, has an online presence and caters to customers all over the world. They identified a need to expand their jewelry selection and cut inventory costs dramatically while maintaining the high quality of their products.

Key Actions and Initiatives:

1. Research and select reliable suppliers:
The store's management conducted extensive research to identify reputable suppliers specializing in dropshipping fine sterling silver and gold jewelry. They focused on suppliers with a strong track record, positive customer reviews, and reasonable pricing. A final selection for a qualified and trusted supplier was finalized.

2. Develop a comprehensive jewelry collection selection:
To offer a wide variety of jewelry products without physical inventory, the store curated a unique and extensive collection of beautifully crafted sterling silver and gold jewelry. They partnered with the identified supplier to source high-quality, exclusive designs that differentiate their store from competitors.

3. Optimize product listings:
The store paid attention to the presentation and appeal of their product listings. They used high-resolution images to showcase the intricate details and craftsmanship of each piece. The product

descriptions were accurate and compelling, emphasizing the quality and uniqueness of the jewelry. Relevant details such as metal type, gemstones, dimensions, and special features were included.

4. Implement effective pricing strategies:
The store analyzed market trends, competitor pricing, and customer preferences to determine optimal price points. They considered the costs associated with dropshipping, such as supplier fees and shipping charges, to ensure they set prices that covered expenses and generated a suitable profit margin. Competitive pricing was maintained while ensuring profitability.

5. Streamline the order fulfillment process:
A seamless process for handling orders was established. Effective communication with their supplier ensured sufficient stock availability and prompt shipping. Inventory management systems were integrated to track product availability and provide real-time updates to customers. Any order issues or delays were addressed promptly to maintain a positive customer experience.

6. Market and promote the store:
A comprehensive marketing strategy was implemented to drive traffic to the online store. The store leveraged various channels such as social media, email marketing, content marketing, and paid advertising to reach their target audience. The unique designs and high quality of the sterling silver and gold jewelry were emphasized to attract customers who valued craftsmanship and style.

7. Analyze data and refine strategies:
The store continuously monitored and analyzed sales data, customer feedback, and market trends. Based on insights obtained, they identified their best-selling items, customer preferences, and opportunities for expansion. The product selection, marketing efforts, and pricing strategies were adjusted accordingly to improve sales and profitability.

Measurable Outcomes:

- The store saw a significant increase in sales due to the expanded jewelry selection and competitive pricing.
- By implementing dropshipping, the store was able to reduce inventory costs, leading to higher overall profitability.
- Customer satisfaction improved as orders were fulfilled promptly, and inventory availability was accurately reflected.
- The store experienced an increase in website traffic and conversions through their comprehensive marketing efforts.
- Continuous analysis and refinement of strategies allowed the store to adapt to changing customer preferences and market trends, further enhancing their success.

Challenges Faced:

- Identifying a reliable supplier was a challenge initially, requiring extensive research and evaluation.
- Maintaining competitive pricing while ensuring profitability was a delicate balance that meant finding real value.
- Promptly addressing any order issues or delays required efficient communication with suppliers and prompt problem-solving.

Lessons Learned:

- Thorough research and careful supplier selection are crucial for dropshipping success.
- Continuous monitoring of market trends and customer preferences is essential for making informed decisions.
- Effective communication with suppliers and prompt problem-solving are vital to maintaining a positive customer experience.

Overall Impact Assessment:

The store successfully maximized the benefits of dropshipping fine jewelry by implementing the discussed dropshipping strategies. Increased sales, reduced inventory costs, and an expanded customer base were achieved. The store's ability to offer a more comprehensive selection of jewelry while maintaining profitability and customer satisfaction was a testament to the effectiveness of their implemented strategies.

Now that we have examined the successful implementation of dropshipping strategies in the case study of Sterling Silver & Gold, it is essential to discuss the key mistakes to avoid in order to replicate their success. By understanding these lessons learned, you can navigate potential challenges and optimize your own dropshipping endeavors.

Typical Mistakes And How To Avoid Them

The mistakes most people make in implementing sterling silver and gold jewelry dropshipping strategies are as follows:

1. Not thoroughly researching and selecting a reliable supplier: It is crucial to research and identify reputable suppliers specializing in dropshipping fine jewelry. Look for suppliers with a strong track record, positive customer reviews, transparency, and reasonable pricing to ensure quality and timely delivery.

2. Failing to develop a comprehensive jewelry design selection: Take advantage of dropshipping by offering a wide variety of jewelry collections without a physical inventory. Curate a unique and extensive collection of high-quality designs to cater to diverse customer preferences and differentiate your store from competitors.

3. Neglecting to optimize product listings: Pay attention to the presentation and appeal of your product listings. Use high-resolution images and write accurate and compelling product descriptions that highlight the quality and uniqueness of the jewelry.

4. Not implementing effective pricing strategies: Analyze market trends, competitor pricing, and customer preferences to determine optimal price points while maintaining profitability.

Consider the costs associated with dropshipping to ensure suitable profit margins.

5. Failing to streamline the order fulfillment process: Establish a seamless approach to handle orders, communicate effectively with suppliers, and integrate inventory management systems. Promptly address any order issues or delays to maintain a positive customer experience.

6. Neglecting to market and promote the store: Implement a comprehensive marketing strategy using various channels such as social media, email marketing, content marketing, and paid advertising. Emphasize the unique designs and high quality of your jewelry to attract customers.

7. Not analyzing data and refining strategies: Continuously monitor and analyze sales data, customer feedback, and market trends. Use these insights to refine your product selection, marketing efforts, and pricing strategies to continually improve sales and profitability.

To avoid these mistakes, conduct thorough research on suppliers, curate a comprehensive product selection, optimize product listings, implement effective pricing strategies, streamline order fulfillment, market and promote your store, and analyze data for continuous improvement. By doing so, you can maximize dropshipping benefits, increase sales, reduce inventory costs, and expand your customer base.

> "Success in the dynamic world of dropshipping requires constant vigilance and adaptability, analyzing sales data, customer feedback, and market trends to refine strategies and stay ahead of the competition."

Now that we have identified the common mistakes to avoid when implementing sterling silver and gold jewelry dropshipping strategies, let me introduce to you my #1 piece of advice.

My #1 Piece Of Advice

Focus on curating a diverse and unique selection of jewelry from an experienced supplier with a minimum of 10 years of dropshipping experience and 25-plus years' experience designing and making jewelry. A manufacturer that has more than 12,000 designs in numerous niche collections to choose from, saving you much time, frustration, and money. You should do this all while keeping inventory costs low by fully embracing the dropshipping model.

Summary:

- Choose a reliable supplier: Research and select a reputable supplier who specializes in dropshipping high-quality jewelry. Look for positive customer reviews and reasonable pricing.
- Curate a unique product selection: Offer a diverse range of beautifully crafted sterling silver and gold jewelry to cater to different customer preferences. Focus on exclusive designs that set your store apart from competitors.
- Optimize jewelry listings: Use high-resolution images and compelling descriptions that emphasize the quality and uniqueness of each piece and the special meaning or stories attached to them. Also, Include relevant details such as metal type, gemstones, and dimensions.
- Implement effective pricing strategies: Analyze market trends and competitor pricing to determine optimal price points. Consider costs associated with dropshipping to ensure profitability while maintaining competitive prices.
- Streamline order fulfillment: Establish a seamless process with suppliers for prompt and efficient shipment of orders. Integrate inventory management systems for real-time updates and promptly address any

issues or delays.

Quiz

1. What is the first step for owners, operators, and managers of sea life jewelry gift shops with online stores to effectively implement the sterling silver and gold jewelry dropshipping strategies?
A. Develop a comprehensive product selection
B. Research and select reliable suppliers
C. Optimize product listings
D. Implement effective pricing strategies

2. What should owners, operators, and managers consider when setting prices for sterling silver and gold jewelry?
A. Market trends
B. Competitor pricing
C. Customer reviews
D. Costs associated with dropshipping

3. What is essential for offering a wide variety of jewelry products without the need for physical inventory?
A. Establishing a seamless order fulfillment process
B. Leveraging various marketing channels
C. Curation of a unique and extensive collection
D. Analysis of customer feedback

4. What should product listings emphasize to attract customers?
A. Intricate details and craftsmanship
B. Reasonable pricing
C. Quality and uniqueness
D. Special features

5. What should be included in the product descriptions?
A. Market trends
B. Metal type
C. Dimensions
D. Gemstones

6. What should owners, operators, and managers analyze to refine their dropshipping strategies?
A. Sales data
B. Inventory costs
C. Market trends
D. Customer preferences

7. What should owners, operators, and managers leverage to reach their target audience?
A. Content marketing
B. Social media
C. Email marketing
D. Paid advertising

8. What should owners, operators, and managers do to ensure the quality, authenticity, and timely delivery of the products?
A. Monitor and analyze customer feedback
B. Track product availability
C. Research and select reliable suppliers
D. Adjust pricing strategies

9. What is the advantage of dropshipping?
A. Selling a wide variety of jewelry products without the need for physical inventory
B. Promptly addressing any order issues or delays
C. Leveraging various marketing channels
D. Offering competitive pricing

10. What should owners, operators, and managers pay attention to when curating a unique and extensive collection of jewelry?
A. Quality and exclusivity of designs
B. Dimensions and gemstones
C. High-resolution images
D. Customer preferences and tastes

***

Answer key:

1. B
2. D
3. C
4. C
5. B, D
6. A, C, D
7. B, C, D
8. C
9. A
10. A

"Now that you understand the key steps involved in implementing the dropshipping strategies for sterling silver and gold jewelry, it's time to review, make notes and take action. Get started expanding your business and streamline the process while cutting costs and increasing profits!

CONCLUSION

Unleash the Power of Ocean Treasures Dropshipping: Revolutionize Your Jewelry Business Today!

Congratulations on completing your journey through "Ocean Treasures Dropshipping: The Ultimate Guide to Making Money with Luxurious Nautical, Sea Life, and Water-sports Jewelry." You now possess a wealth of knowledge that will empower you to transform your struggling dive, ocean sports, marina gift, and jewelry ocean/beach resort shops/stores into thriving online businesses. With a focus on mid-level to high-end ocean sports, sea life, and nautical retail jewelry, this guide has equipped you with practical advice, tips, tricks, and examples to help you dominate the market and skyrocket your online sales.

Embrace the Power of Wide Jewelry Collection Selections:

One of the key takeaways from our journey together is the importance of offering your customers a wide selection of jewelry. By expanding your range of jewelry collections, you not only cater to a broader audience but also increase your chances of getting noticed in a highly competitive market. With dropshipping, you can effortlessly expand and add massive value to your online store, offering extensive collections in sterling silver and gold jewelry that captivates your customers and keeps them coming back for more.

Escape the Burdens of Inventory Control:

One of the biggest challenges faced by jewelry store owners is inventory management. It often consumes precious time and resources, leaving little room for business expansion. Fortunately, with dropshipping, this burden becomes a thing of the past. By partnering with a reputable jewelry manufacturer, you can divert your attention to other critical aspects of running your business while leaving the hassle of inventory control behind. This newfound freedom will allow you to focus on what you do best: driving sales and growing your brand.

Overcome Cash Flow Challenges:

Managing tight cash flow is a common struggle for many jewelry business owners. Traditional methods often require significant upfront investments to maintain inventory levels and cover operational costs. Thankfully, dropshipping eliminates these financial constraints. By partnering with a reputable jewelry manufacturer that handles the production and shipment of products, you free up capital that would otherwise be tied up in an inventory. This flexibility empowers you to allocate resources more efficiently, reinvesting in marketing initiatives, customer engagement, and business growth.

The Embrace of Online Sales:

As we have emphasized throughout our journey, the future of retail lies within the digital realm. The ever-expanding online marketplace offers unparalleled opportunities for your jewelry business to thrive. With the knowledge gained from this guide, you now possess the tools to create a compelling online presence, attract a loyal customer base, and drive exponential growth. Harness the power of social media marketing, utilize search engine optimization (SEO) techniques, and provide an exceptional user experience to ensure your online store remains at the forefront of the industry.

Take Action Today:

Now is the time to put your newfound knowledge and insights into action. You possess the expertise necessary to revolutionize your jewelry business and drive it towards unprecedented success. To break free from the burdens of the jeweler's workbench, take the next step and hop on a call with a qualified and reputable jewelry manufacturer. By partnering with experienced professionals who have served hundreds of independent designers and artists worldwide, you can unlock new levels of efficiency and creativity, ultimately propelling your business to greater heights.

"Ocean Treasures Dropshipping: The Ultimate Guide to Making Money with Luxurious Nautical, Sea Life, and Water-sports Jewelry" has equipped you with the strategies and know-how to transform your struggling dive, ocean sports, marina gift, and jewelry ocean/beach resort shops/stores into flourishing online ventures. By embracing dropshipping, widening your selection, freeing yourself from inventory control, and leveraging the power of online sales, you are positioned to dominate the market. Reinvent your business today and embark on a journey to redefine your success in the online niche jewelry markets of your choice.

Remember, the ocean is vast, and within it lies endless treasures waiting to be discovered. Embrace the power of dropshipping, seize control of your future, and sail towards a prosperous and fulfilling jewelry business. The time to act is now!

Hop on that call and unlock the potential within you. The ocean awaits.

Book your Discovery Call here _____link_____

Wishing you smooth sailing and soaring profits,

Peter Stone

Glossary - Definitions + Context

Dropshipping: a retail fulfillment method where a store doesn't keep the products it sells in stock and instead transfers the customer orders and shipment details to a wholesaler or manufacturer who then ships the goods directly to the customer.

Context: Dropshipping is essential for struggling owners, operators, and managers of dive, surf, ocean sports, and beach resort sea life jewelry gift shops with online stores. It eliminates the need to hold inventory, reducing inventory costs and eliminating the risk of inventory overstock. It also offers the opportunity to expand the business by delivering unique, in-demand jewelry worldwide, resulting in increased sales and a bigger online store presence.

Inventory Overstock: a situation where a business has excessive stock of certain items that are not selling as expected.

Context: Inventory overstock can be problematic for owners and managers of jewelry gift shops with online stores. It ties up capital in unsold products, increases storage costs, and hampers cash flow. By implementing a dropshipping service, the risk of inventory overstock is mitigated, allowing the business to have better control over their inventory levels and focus on selling the most in-demand items.

Worldwide Delivery: the ability to ship products to customers in different countries and regions.

Context: For owners and managers of dive, surf, ocean sports, and beach resort sea life jewelry gift shops with online stores, offering worldwide delivery is crucial. It expands the potential sales market and opens up opportunities for global customers to purchase their unique jewelry products. With dropshipping, the business can effortlessly fulfill orders from customers around the world, expanding their reach and increasing sales.

Virtual Inventory: a concept where products are displayed on an online store but are not physically stocked by the business. Instead, they are sourced and shipped directly by a third-party supplier.

Context: Implementing a dropshipping service allows for the creation of a virtual inventory. This virtual inventory eliminates the need for the struggling owner, operator, or manager to invest in holding physical inventory, reducing costs associated with inventory storage, management, and transportation. It also provides the flexibility to easily update and expand the product range without the constraints of physical space.

Unique Jewelry Images: high-quality visual representations of the jewelry products that are distinctive, appealing, and exclusive to the business.

Context: In the competitive world of online retail, having unique jewelry images is vital. Struggling owners, operators, and managers need to differentiate their products and stand out from the competition to attract potential customers. By offering visually captivating and exclusive product images, the business can increase its online store presence, capture the attention of customers, and drive sales.

Sea Life: a term referring to the diverse range of aquatic organisms and ecosystems found in oceans, seas, and other bodies of saltwater.

Context: The focus of the struggling owners, operators, and managers is on dive, surf, ocean sports, and beach resort sea life-related jewelry gift shops. It is essential to understand and appreciate the significance of sea life in their product offerings. By showcasing sea life-inspired or themed jewelry, the business can connect with customers who have a particular interest or affinity for the ocean, thereby increasing the potential for sales and customer satisfaction.

Online Data Analysis: the systematic examination and interpretation of data collected from various online sources to gain insights, identify patterns, and make informed business decisions.

Context: For owners and managers of online stores, conducting online data analysis is imperative. It allows them to understand customer behavior, identify trends, and optimize their marketing and sales strategies. Effective data analysis can help struggling owners identify customer preferences, focus on high-potential sales products, and enhance their overall business performance.

Active Sales: the process of proactively engaging with customers, nurturing leads, and actively pursuing sales opportunities.

Context: Struggling owners, operators, and managers cannot solely rely on passive marketing techniques to drive sales. By actively engaging with customers, offering personalized recommendations, and providing excellent customer service, the business can increase their chances of converting potential sales. Active sales efforts, combined with an extensive selection of jewelry products and a reliable dropshipping service, can significantly improve sales revenue and overall business growth.

Potential Sales: the estimated number or value of sales that could be achieved in a specific period or under certain circumstances.

Context: Recognizing and capitalizing on potential sales

opportunities is crucial for struggling owners, operators, and managers. By offering a wide range of high-quality sea life and nautical-themed jewelry, coupled with a global dropshipping service, the business can tap into a broader customer base and increase the potential for sales. Identifying and targeting such potential sales can significantly contribute to the growth and success of the business.

Dead Inventory Costs: the expenses associated with holding and managing unsold or stagnant inventory.

Context: Dead inventory can be a significant financial burden for struggling owners, operators, and managers. It ties up capital, incurs storage costs, and prevents the business from investing in more profitable inventory. By implementing a dropshipping service, the business can reduce dead inventory costs since they only purchase products from suppliers when a customer places an order. This eliminates the risk of possessing dead stock and allows the business to redirect resources towards more lucrative opportunities.

Is this The Back Cover?

"Expand Your Reach & Skyrocket Your Online Sales with Unique Designs in Beautifully Crafted Fine Sterling Silver and 14, 18 and 22 Kt Gold Jewelry"

Dreaming of expanding your business but don't want to deal with the hassles of inventory control and cash flow? Now you can make a big splash with a unique yet simple and profitable, deliver anywhere, dropshipping jewelry program.

Unique Designs in Beautifully Crafted Fine Sterling Silver and 14, 18 or 22 Kt Gold Jewelry is your gateway to reaching a global market with an exceptionally wide choice of sea life, water sports, and nautical jewelry designs. Our dropship program eliminates inventory constraints and tight cash flow, giving you the freedom to focus on what matters most: growing your business.

No more cramped quarters. No more late nights spent counting inventory. Just the freedom to reach your customers wherever they are in the world. With unique designs in beautifully crafted fine precious metals jewelry, you can be sure to make a huge impact on the market and skyrocket your online sales worldwide.

Stop dreaming and start doing. Buy a copy of this book to change your life's pathway for increased prosperity, abundance, and brand awareness. Unique Designs in Beautifully Crafted Fine Sterling Silver And 14, 18 And 22 Kt Gold Jewelry is the perfect way to take your business to the next level.

www.ingramcontent.com/pod-product-compliance
Lightning Source LLC
Chambersburg PA
CBHW072213290526
45794CB00004B/1742